HOW TO GROW FLOWERS
in
SMALL SPACES

*An Illustrated Guide to
Planning, Planting, and Caring for
Your Small Space Flower Garden*

STEPHANIE WALKER

ADAMS MEDIA
New York London Toronto Sydney New Delhi

Adams Media
An Imprint of Simon & Schuster, LLC
100 Technology Center Drive
Stoughton, Massachusetts 02072

First Adams Media hardcover edition April 2024

ADAMS MEDIA and colophon are registered trademarks of Simon & Schuster, LLC.

Simon & Schuster: Celebrating 100 Years of Publishing in 2024

For information about special discounts for bulk purchases, please contact Simon & Schuster Special Sales at 1-866-506-1949 or business@simonandschuster.com.

The Simon & Schuster Speakers Bureau can bring authors to your live event. For more information or to book an event, contact the Simon & Schuster Speakers Bureau at 1-866-248-3049 or visit our website at www.simonspeakers.com.

Interior design by Priscilla Yuen
Illustrations by Nicola Cunneen
Interior images © 123RF/Algirdas Urbonavicius, Anna Kutukova, roystudio; Simon & Schuster, LLC

Manufactured in China

10   9   8   7   6   5   4   3   2   1

Library of Congress Cataloging-in-Publication Data
Names: Walker, Stephanie (Gardener), author.
Title: How to grow flowers in small spaces / Stephanie Walker.
Other titles: Illustrated guide to planning, planting, and caring for your small space flower garden
Description: Stoughton, Massachusetts: Adams Media, 2024. | Includes bibliographical references and index.
Identifiers: LCCN 2023024291 | ISBN 9781507220481 (hc) | ISBN 9781507220498 (ebook)
Subjects: LCSH: Flower gardening. | Container gardening. | Small gardens. | Handbooks and manuals.
Classification: LCC SB405 .W27 2024 | DDC 635.9--dc23/eng/20230825
LC record available at https://lccn.loc.gov/2023024291

ISBN 978-1-5072-2048-1
ISBN 978-1-5072-2049-8 (ebook)

For Chris:
My sunshine, soil, and water.
May we garden together until the sun sets.

For Quincy, Ellie, and Rees:
The best and most favorite things I've ever grown.
May you always know where to set your roots.

For you, my flower friend:
May life's winds blow only wildflower seeds your way.

And for Aunt Camilla, who planted the seed.

Contents

Introduction

Do you love flowers but feel like you might not have the skills, time, or knowledge to grow them yourself? Do you find yourself just going to buy flowers from your favorite florist because you think it will be too hard to grow your own? Maybe you only have a small outdoor space (or possibly even none!) and don't know where to start a flower garden? The good news is that you can grow your own beautiful flowers in the space you have, and it might even be easier than you think!

How to Grow Flowers in Small Spaces will give you the knowledge and advice you need to grow your own stunning flowers. In this book you'll learn how to:

- Prepare your space and soil
- Design your garden (no matter the size!)
- Pick the correct containers for the plants you choose
- Cultivate and tend to your flowers
- Harvest your flowers

In addition, you'll discover the best practices for irrigating your plants, resources for discovering the best planting times and plants for your area, and why recording everything is vital to a bountiful garden year after year. You will also learn about the importance of feeding your soil and techniques for successful seed starting, both outside and indoors.

You'll also find detailed information on forty popular varieties of flowers that are some of the easiest to grow, ideal for cutting, and can grow in almost all planting zones. In addition, each flower entry will include illustrations, in-depth growing instructions, and tips. With valuable information about plant placement, garden bed layouts, and troubleshooting tricks and tips, growing flowers in containers, yards, and small spaces has never been easier.

Create your own garden masterpiece....It's time to start growing!

How to Use This Book

Whether you are a novice or professional, this book will walk you through the process and help you map out your garden so that it will produce precisely what you want. In Chapter 6 you will find a detailed list of forty different flowers, with specific information on how to grow and care for them and when to harvest them. Within each flower description, you will find useful advice on growing flowers in containers and which plants are best suited for containers, along with suggestions on the size of container for each flower. Before you jump ahead, though, take time to learn how to choose the perfect location for your flower garden and how to set up your garden beds or containers for success.

Each flower variety listed in Chapter 6 is categorized by how difficult they are to grow. Under the "Difficulty" section for each plant, three levels are listed:

LEVEL 1: EASY

From bachelor's buttons to lilacs, these flowers are simple to grow and have the fewest steps from planting to harvest.

LEVEL 2: MEDIUM

From Asiatic lilies to peonies, these flowers may have a couple of extra steps required for growing success—and there are things like pests to look out for along the way.

LEVEL 3: DIFFICULT

From dahlias to roses, these flowers can be difficult to grow for various reasons—but don't be afraid to give them a try! Level 3 flowers require more effort, but everything you need to know is included in the entry. Read the growing information carefully and follow each step to be successful.

Remember, don't be alarmed by the difficulty level of a certain flower—no matter what the level, if you follow the information relevant to each flower, you can grow them successfully.

In addition, included in Appendix A are four sample garden layouts that you can use as a template to grow in your own yard. These layouts are suggestions of flower varieties that work well together and grow in similar seasons. As you become more familiar with each flower, you can begin to make substitutions to benefit your specific tastes and growing conditions.

If your goal is to grow flowers to bring into your home, you will find Appendix B especially helpful. This appendix teaches the basics of arranging bouquets with a useful chart to help explain how to use each flower.

Chapter 1

Getting Started

The thought of growing flowers may seem a bit overwhelming at first, but with a little understanding of basic gardening principles, you can grow amazing florist shop-quality flowers in your very own yard and containers. Whether you are a beginner or advanced gardener, you can have a beautiful, thriving flower garden. This chapter will explain some of the benefits to flower gardening and teach you how to get started.

Also in this chapter, you'll learn how growing flowers benefits your emotional and physical health as well as the environment around you. You'll also discover the importance of establishing a plan and selecting the best location for your garden bed, along with best watering practices. As you get started with your garden and your flowers begin blooming, you will experience the joy that flowers can bring!

The Benefits of Flower Gardening

Besides creating a beautiful environment, growing your own flowers can benefit you mentally and physically. This section will explore the numerous benefits of flower gardening and what it can do for you.

GROWING FLOWERS CAN IMPROVE YOUR MOOD

Many gardeners refer to their garden space as their "happy place," but did you know that there is scientific evidence to support the claim that gardening can actually improve your mood, thus becoming a literal happy place? The connection we have with plants is so strong that it takes less than 20 minutes in their presence to elevate our mood.

In addition, the simple act of digging in the dirt stirs up microbes in the soil. When these microbes are inhaled, serotonin production is stimulated. These microbes, known as *Mycobacterium vaccae*, have been found to mimic the effect on neurons that antidepressant drugs provide. This bacterium stimulates serotonin production, causing you to relax and feel happier. As your body responds to this serotonin boost, your mood elevates, stress is released, and your body is able to relax and enjoy your surroundings.

Spending a few minutes each day outdoors tending to your garden space can have a grounding effect and allow you to release stress that builds up as you go about your day-to-day activities.

As you tend to your garden, you are able to redirect any stress you may be feeling and refocus your energy to something that returns growth energy.

GARDENING INCREASES PHYSICAL ACTIVITY

Gardening is an activity that requires movement and therefore increases your heart rate and causes you to engage muscle groups in new ways. As you bend down to weed, dig, and plant, you are stretching and strengthening muscles. When you rake or shovel compost, you are elevating your heart rate and providing much-needed cardio exercise for your body. All these activities lead to greater physical capacity and endurance. As you continually garden, you will feel your body growing stronger and your lung capacity and stamina improving.

GARDENS ENCOURAGE POLLINATORS

Pollinators (an insect or other agent that transfers pollen from one plant to another) are essential to plant reproduction. The plant uses the pollen to produce a fruit or seed. Without the aid of a pollinator, many plants would not be able to reproduce. Bees are the most common pollinator, with over twenty thousand species of wild bees, but they are not the only pollinators. Other important contributors are butterflies, wasps, beetles, moths, and hummingbirds. As your plants grow and your flowers begin to bloom, you will notice that beneficial pollinators are attracted to your garden. As these pollinators move from blossom to blossom, they are spreading pollen vital to plant reproduction. It is essential that you welcome these important workers to your garden and even encourage them by creating spaces that can sustain them. Consider including a small birdbath in your garden to allow pollinators a place to obtain water vital to their hydration. You could also provide a pollinator habitat for them to inhabit.

GROWING FLOWERS IMPROVES YOUR SOIL

As you plant and grow flowers, the roots of those plants work to loosen the soil around them to allow for oxygen and water movement within the soil. As they do so, they take up and deposit nutrients into the soil. As the flower grows and matures, often it will shed leaves that provide nutrients to the soil if left to decompose where they drop.

When you are changing out a garden bed after a growing season has finished, consider cutting your plant at the base and leaving the roots in the soil instead of pulling the entire plant. By doing so, you are not disturbing the growing system the plant has established, and you are leaving the roots to decompose in the ground to provide living matter to feed the soil to benefit whatever you plant next. This can be true for container gardening as well. However, it is sometimes best to pull out the entire plant since container space is limited and it may be difficult to plant around the roots that have been left in the container.

Set Yourself Up for Success

In order to succeed at growing, you must first try to grow something. And to be honest, you will fail at gardening sometimes. But at other times, you will experience the most exciting success. Hopefully, you can commit to getting back up and trying again after you fail. Let's explore some of the ways to set yourself up for success in growing.

GROW AT THE RIGHT TIME FOR YOUR AREA

There are few things more frustrating than planting a flower only to watch it die shortly after planting. When a flower plant dies, the first thing to do is to diagnose why. One of the most common reasons a flower dies is that it was planted at the wrong time for your area. Every plant has a season in which it grows best. You can determine that season by consulting your local county extension planting calendar and planting accordingly. (For more information on this, see Chapter 4.)

CREATE A PLAN

It is important to determine the best steps for your particular garden before you even begin planting. First, you'll need to decide if you are going to sow seeds on your own indoors, if you are going to direct sow your seeds, or if you are going to purchase transplants from your local garden center or nursery. To sow a seed is simply the process of planting a seed. Direct sowing is the practice of planting seeds directly into the soil or container rather than planting by transplant. A transplant is a seed that has been started ahead of time, allowed to grow, and then the entire plant is planted into a space. Factors that might be helpful in determining which course of action you should follow are:

- If you are really on top of things and look a month or two ahead on your local growing calendar, starting seeds indoors is a great option because it will give you a jump start on growing and will put you ahead of schedule when you plant your transplant outside. Plus, starting your own seeds indoors to be transplanted later saves you money.

- If you are on time with your local growing calendar, direct sowing seeds is a great option and can often save you money.

- If you are behind schedule with your local growing calendar, purchasing transplants is a great option because it will catch you up with time you may have missed trying to germinate (sprout a plant from seed) in the ground. Germination occurs as soon as growth from the seed is evident. However, purchasing transplants can be expensive.

Each of these methods would be acceptable in a container gardening situation. Direct sowing seeds in containers can be successful and reduce the risk of transplant shock, which is stress that occurs in a plant after it has been recently planted. Starting seeds indoors for transplanting later or purchasing transplants can also be successful in container gardening. Planting transplants in your containers will provide instant color and foliage. If you choose to direct sow seeds in your containers, keep in mind that you will not have instant foliage or color, as you will have to wait as your seedlings (young plants grown from seed) germinate and grow. Whichever method you choose for your containers, you will find success as you follow the principles outlined in this book.

SELECT A SITE

It is important to consciously select the best area of your yard to plant certain

flowers because sunlight is absolutely essential in growing healthy flowers. Paying attention to the amount of sun particular flowers require will ensure the success of the plant. Roses, for example, should have 6–8 hours of sunlight per day in order to perform their best. (You will find sunlight requirements specific to forty select flowers in Chapter 6.)

An easy way to determine the amount of sun any given area of your yard receives is to track the sun throughout the day. If you are growing in containers, follow these same steps to ensure your plants receive adequate sunlight. Keep in mind that when you grow in containers, you have the freedom to move your plants throughout the day to provide them with ample sunlight or to protect them from too much sunlight. If your pots are extra heavy, place them on plant stands with wheels to enable moving them around as needed. Use these steps to track the sunlight in your yard:

1 Pick a day where you will be home all day, and track the sunlight from 6:00 a.m. to 6:00 p.m.

2 Divide your yard into a grid of manageable sections.

3 At 6:00 a.m. begin observing the amount of sunlight each section of your yard receives by making a note in each section of how the sun

is lighting that area. For example, if you notice a section is full of sunlight and no shade, mark it as full sun. If a section is shaded by your house, your neighbor's house, or a fence, mark it as shade. If a section has some sunlight filtering through due to a tree, mark it as partial shade.

4 Set an alarm for each subsequent hour of the day and repeat the process hourly until 6:00 p.m.

5 Tally up the amount of sun for each section. If an area was in full sun from 6:00 a.m. until 10:00 a.m., shaded from 11:00 a.m. until 3:00 p.m., and then sun again from 3:00 p.m. until 6:00 p.m., that area received 7 total hours of sunlight that day. Notice that you are looking for total hours of sunlight per day, not consecutive hours of sunlight per day.

6 Create a garden plan incorporating the plants and flowers you desire, noting the best areas of your yard to plant them according to the amount of sunlight available in each area.

Keep in mind that the sun's patterns change throughout the year depending on the season. You may need to repeat this process a couple times throughout the year (or even as your trees grow)

to account for the changing seasons. If a plant requires full sun, that amount equates to at least 6 hours of sunlight per day. Partial shade is an area that receives less than 3 hours of direct sunlight per day.

PREP YOUR SOIL

Since soil is one of the foundational elements required by all plants, it is important to have healthy soil. Whenever you can, take the opportunity to improve your soil. Remember to feed your soil with organic matter so your soil can feed your plants. Organic practices include planting or treating plants without the aid of chemical fertilizers, pesticides, or other artificial agents. Adding organic matter to your garden beds or mixing it into containers provides a slow release of nutrients over the growing season as the matter breaks down. Natural and organic fertilizers feed the soil's living organisms, who break down these fertilizers into nutrients the plants can use. (This is discussed more in depth in Chapter 5.) Paying attention to the health of your soil will pay big dividends. In other words, don't treat your soil like dirt!

Special attention should be paid to any plants grown in containers. As plants grow in pots, they are using up all the available nutrients within that pot since they are not able to access anything outside of the container. Unless you are adding constant nutrients, the soil will become depleted quickly. It is a good idea to replace the soil in potted plants every 12–18 months. If the soil in your pot becomes hard, it should be replaced as well. A good rule to follow is to amend your soil whenever you plant something new, whether in the ground or in a container. (You can find more information on amending soil in Chapter 3.) As you do this, the health of your soil improves, and the quality of your flowers increases. In fact, healthy soil will even deter pests! (More on this in Chapter 3.)

PLAN YOUR IRRIGATION

Watering your plants, also known as irrigation, is an essential element in growing flowers. Before planting, it is important to determine how your flowers will be irrigated. Consistent irrigation will produce lush, tall plants with bigger and healthier blooms. It is especially important to plan for and monitor your container-grown plants as their water needs will differ from anything planted in the ground. Addressing watering needs before you begin planting will remove much of the headache that comes with a poorly planned watering method. You'll learn more about watering methods in Chapter 2.

CREATE A GARDEN JOURNAL

If you are a natural record-keeper, garden journaling will come easy to you.

If you are not, find a way to become a record-keeper. Keeping record of what you are doing and observing in your garden will prove invaluable from year to year. Even if you have an excellent memory, you will find that it becomes difficult to remember many of the important aspects of gardening. Creating a journal page for each month is beneficial as you track the happenings in your garden and gives you something to look back on from year to year.

Some of the important things to take note of are:

- What you are planting
- When you planted it
- How you planted it (direct sow, used transplants that you purchased, started seeds indoors)
- Soil conditions and amendments (organic matter added to improve the condition of the soil)
- Types and composition of containers
- Whether you replaced or amended the soil in your container
- Seasonal watering needs of your container-grown plants
- Diseases your plants suffered
- Monthly expenditures/costs of specific plants or garden items
- Temperature and general weather conditions
- Pests (destructive insects that harm, attack, or destroy plants) that you observed in your garden

- Beneficial insects (any set of species of pests that perform important tasks, such as pollination or pest control) in your garden
- When you first noticed a germinated seed
- Date of your first bloom on each plant
- Date of your first harvested bloom on each plant

- Tasks/goals for the month
- Highlights
- Lowlights
- Favorite varieties
- Any other relevant notes

Now that you have selected your spot and prepared your soil, it's time to start planning your garden and deciding what types of flowers to plant.

Chapter 2

Planning Your Flower Garden

One way to avoid the stress that can accompany gardening is to take time to plan your garden. Planning your garden from the beginning provides you with a road map to follow and takes the guesswork out of gardening. When you make it a priority to design and create your growing space, seasonal planting becomes a breeze. As you take a few moments each month to consult your local growing calendar (consult Chapter 4 for more information on this) and consciously consider what you would like to accomplish that month, the task of gardening becomes easier and more enjoyable. This chapter focuses on the important tasks to consider when planning your garden.

Considerations for Growing in a Small Space

What happens if you don't have a yard to plant? Consider planting in containers. You need not be denied the beauty of flowers simply because you don't have a yard. Find a spot on your porch or balcony to accommodate size-appropriate containers and get to work. Consult Chapter 6 to discover plants that perform well in containers and even those flowers that perform well indoors.

One technique you could incorporate in your small space is to grow vertically. Consider training a climbing rose up a trellis around your doorway or on your patio. Vertical gardening increases your growing space and provides interest and beauty to your home.

In addition, because you are growing in a small space, try growing dwarf varieties of the flowers you love. Regular zinnias can get tall and unruly and can overtake a small space quickly, but their dwarf varieties are perfect for a container on a doorstep or front stoop.

Choosing the Perfect Container

There are many different types and sizes of containers for planting. Containers can be made of terra-cotta, plastic, ceramic, wood, metal, stone, concrete, or hanging baskets lined with coconut coir. Each of these materials presents a different personality when it comes to having something planted in it. Terra-cotta is porous and will cause the soil to dry out more quickly as the moisture is able to evaporate more easily. Metal can become hot as the sun beats on it. No matter the container type, it is important to monitor it and determine what the water needs will be, keeping in mind that these needs will change from season to season and container to container.

Mapping Out Your Garden Space

The first step in garden planning is to select exactly where you will be planting your flower gardens. Since you have already mapped the sun's patterns in your yard (see Chapter 1), you know exactly how much sun each area of your space receives, and you can select flowers that do best in each situation (consult Chapter 6). Knowing this information will help you determine what plants to grow in each area. For example, if you have an area that is predominately shaded throughout the day, consider planting flowers and plants that thrive in shady environments in that location.

Now you can begin to map out the shape for each garden bed according to the sunlight each area receives. Use graph paper to sketch out a rough design of your yard and the growing spaces you would like to incorporate within your space. Sketch each space so you know roughly the amount of space your flowers will take up and how much space you have to fill. You will find growth dimensions of specific flowers in Chapter 6.

If you are primarily gardening in containers, you have the freedom and ability to be creative in arranging your containers. Consider using containers of varying heights or even placing your containers on a stairstep or circular stand. This will give your plants dimension while presenting them in the best way possible. It will also be visually pleasing while utilizing your space efficiently. Additionally, you could employ hanging planters in a patio space or along fences and walls.

Determining Your Irrigation Method

Since water is one of the most important elements in growing plants, setting up a consistent irrigation method for your flower garden before planting anything is crucial to the success of your garden. Now that you have sketched your garden areas, you know exactly where you need to incorporate irrigation.

If you are able, setting your watering system to turn on automatically will give you the best results in your garden. You can install a watering system that will handle your entire yard and garden area, or you can purchase individual timers to connect to your garden hose. These are battery operated and can be set manually or controlled through Bluetooth. There are many methods for watering, and this section will discuss some that you may want to consider. Then you can choose the method that works for you.

DRIP IRRIGATION

Drip irrigation is the practice of placing rubber tubing with emitters on the ground near the base of your plant. This method of watering plants is effective and saves water by facilitating deep and less frequent watering. The emitters will slowly drip water into the soil at the root zone. As your plant grows, you can move the drip line farther from the plant to allow it to drip to the growing root system. Emitters can be adjusted according to the amount of water you desire for a specific plant, and you can purchase emitters that have various rates of output. Utilizing drip irrigation is ideal because it allows you to water your plants directly. Drip irrigation is especially effective in container-planted flowers. You can simply run a line to each container with an emitter that is suitable for the size of the

container and needs of the plant. As you use this method, you will see your plant quality and productivity improve.

SOAKER HOSE

A soaker hose looks much like a typical garden hose, but instead of being a solid rubber hose, it is porous to allow water to slowly seep from it. This slow, seeping action facilitates even watering of plants in your garden. Soaker hoses can be strategically placed in your garden to optimize watering efforts and are efficient since the water is dripping directly at the base of the plants, thus reducing water waste from overspray. Soaker hoses are easy to move around to different areas of the garden and can even be hooked up to timers.

MICRO-SPRINKLER

A micro-sprinkler is just what the name implies: a tiny sprinkler. Comparable to sprinklers used in watering your lawn, they emit a spraying pattern of water where the radius can be adjusted to cover up to 360 degrees. Micro-sprinklers can be an effective option when you need to water a larger garden area than what a drip emitter will allow. The spray from a micro-sprinkler can water a 3'–5' radius.

Micro-sprinklers are installed on a length of spaghetti tubing, or very small tubing used in the irrigation of plants, similar to how drip emitters are installed. One benefit of micro-sprinklers is that they can be moved and directed at certain areas of your garden. If you have an area that has greater water needs, and you need to cover a larger area than what a drip emitter will cover, these sprinklers are a great option. Similarly, if you have one plant with greater water needs, you can direct a single micro-sprinkler to that plant. Another benefit is that you can adjust the water output on micro-sprinklers.

OLLAS

Ollas are unglazed clay pots that are buried in the ground or in containers near the roots of your plants, filled with water, and then allowed to water plants as the plant roots draw water as needed through the clay of the pot. This is an excellent watering method for container-grown plants. If using ollas in containers, however, be sure to account for the space they take up as you are planning what to plant in your container. Ollas should be monitored to ensure that as they run out of water, they are refilled.

HAND WATERING

Watering by hand is the most time-consuming of all the methods of watering since you are responsible for doing it yourself. However, many people enjoy this garden task as it gives them time to be in their garden, observing what is growing and noticing problems that might need solving. One drawback to relying on hand watering as the sole means of water for your container or garden is that it ties you to the garden. If you are not able to water for a day or two, you run the risk of plants dying that you have invested time planting, cultivating, and caring for. This can be frustrating and often leads people to give up on gardening. When possible, it is always best to automate your watering.

RAIN

Rain is an effective watering method if you live in an area that is blessed by rain. If you live in a drier climate and cannot rely on rain as a consistent watering method, consider capturing the rain that does fall in rain-harvesting tanks. In fact, in any climate, harvesting rainwater is a great way to conserve resources. Consult your local authorities for laws regarding the harvesting of rain.

If your containers are in a partially covered area, such as a patio, you can get creative in the ways that you capture rain for them. If you are able, simply move your containers into the rain to collect the water that falls. If moving your containers is not an option, you may be able to hang a bucket from a balcony to gather rain that you can then use to water your plants. Or you can brainstorm other creative methods of collecting this precious resource.

When and How Long to Water

Once you've decided which irrigation method best suits your garden, it is important to determine when and how long to water. Follow these simple watering steps:

1 Once you have planted your seed, keep the soil moist until it germinates. This might mean watering the area multiple times a day to keep the seed from drying out.

2 Once germinated, or if planting a transplant, water daily (sometimes a couple times a day) until your seedling or transplant is established. A plant is established when the newly planted plant shows new growth and the roots have anchored themselves into the soil. This usually takes 1–2 weeks.

3 Once established, water when the top 1" of soil is dry.

4 To measure water depth, wait 30 minutes after watering and then probe the soil with a soil probe, long screwdriver, or your finger to see how far the water has penetrated. A soil probe is a metal shaft that is pushed into the ground to determine the depth of moisture in the soil, especially after irrigation has occurred or when attempting to determine if a plant needs water.

Water vegetables and flowers to a depth of 6"–12". Water shrubs and bushes to a depth of 18"–24". Water trees to a depth of 3'.

5 If water has not reached desired depth, turn on the water to that plant and continue the same procedure until desired depth is achieved.

6 Adjust your watering schedule seasonally as temperatures change and according to the needs of your plants as you observe them.

Obviously, the watering needs of your containers will differ from anything planted in the ground. Potted plants need moist, well-draining soil. Fortunately, many of the potting soil mixes that are available today are designed for good drainage while at the same time providing for moisture retention. When watering your potted plants, it is just as important not to overwater them as it is to underwater them.

To know when to water, simply stick your finger into the soil of the potted plant to see how dry or wet it is. You should water your plant when it feels dry 2" below the surface. Keep in mind that in containers, soil moisture levels change more rapidly than in something that is planted in the ground. Soil that feels moist in the morning may be dry by the afternoon.

Selecting What to Plant

Now that you have established your growing beds and provided them with water, you can begin plant selection. Spend a little time looking through the flowers in Chapter 6 and decide what you want to plant. Select plants according to the amount of sun the area receives throughout the day. Be sure to select and plant plants in the correct growing season for that particular plant. (Consult Chapter 4 for growing calendar information.) If you live in a warmer climate, you may be able to start some flowers in the fall that others are not able to plant until the spring.

DESIGNING YOUR FLOWER BEDS

Be prepared to organize your plants in a manner that will put them on the best display. A trick to accomplishing this is arranging them by height. If your garden spot is against a fence or wall, organize your plants with the flowers with the tallest potential nearest the fence or wall and scaling down in potential height as they get closer to the yard area of the garden. In this manner of planting, you will have a background flower, middle flower, and foreground flower. (Refer to the Flower Planting Game Plan chart in Appendix B.)

If your planting area is in the middle of a yard or a spot that will be walked around on all sides, consider planting flowers that will achieve the tallest height in the middle of the garden bed and tapering down, with the shortest flowers nearest the area people are walking around.

As you are planning your garden beds, plan on incorporating some perennial plants in your landscape, some annual plants, and some biennial plants.

- A perennial is a plant that lives and blooms for more than 2 years.

- An annual is a plant that completes its growing cycle from seed to bloom to seed production and then dies all in one season.

- A biennial is a flowering plant that takes 2 years to complete its growth cycle, typically growing foliage the first year and blooming the second year.

You should plan on planting annuals every year, unless they are reseeders—in which case, they will take care of planting themselves for you. Reseeding is the process by which a flower produces seed and then drops the seed to germinate and return the following year. As you become more proficient in flower gardening, you will learn to plan ahead and start your own seeds for these annual flowers indoors in anticipation of the coming growing season.

These same guidelines would apply to growing in containers as well. Consider arranging your plants by height to create the greatest visual interest. You might even find it fun to plant your containers by color, and then you have the freedom to mix and mingle your plants to design beautiful, themed container gardens. Imagine planting in all the colors of the rainbow and arranging your containers accordingly. Alternatively, you could arrange your containers for a special holiday, or you could plan for a moon garden by planting containers of whites and silvers that would make an astonishing display at night. The possibilities are endless!

ADDING INTEREST

Of course you would love a beautiful garden full of flowers, but you also need to have something to look at within the garden. Have you thought of adding benches to your gardens so that you have a place to sit and enjoy this space you have worked so hard to cultivate? Providing an area of respite to rest and meditate aids in regenerating mental health in the midst of a beautiful space. You might enjoy dedicating a small corner of your garden to the fairies by creating a tiny fairy garden.

Depending on the space available in your garden, some other elements you might consider adding are:

- Fountains
- Birdbaths
- Birdhouses
- Statues
- Gazing balls
- Armillary spheres
- Arbors and trellises
- Paths
- Stepping stones
- Lights
- Hammocks
- Elements of whimsy

Structural elements such as those previously listed are inviting and draw the eye to a particular space. Much like a work of art, gardens encourage reflection, meditation, and elicit feelings of joy and satisfaction. Even in small spaces there can be room for these decorative elements that can have a big impact. However you decide to design and decorate your garden, be sure to add just enough of your personality to it. After all, you've put so much time into preparing, creating, and designing it that it should reflect its creator.

Chapter 3

Preparing Your Garden Beds

Now that you have planned your garden, you have a clear vision of the look you want to achieve in your garden and so you can begin preparing your growing beds. Since you have figured out the location of your beds and your watering system, preparing your beds for planting will be simple. This chapter discusses how to prepare your beds and establish soil that is so healthy it actually deters pests. You will also find tips and tricks for container gardening and how to prepare your containers for planting.

Establishing Your Garden Bed

If your flower plants are going to succeed and produce big, beautiful blooms, you need to make sure that they are comfortable in their beds. As you establish and create your growing bed, there are a few things you should do to make sure that your flowers are supported in their growing space.

REMOVE ROCKS

First, clear the growing bed of rocks. You want to ensure that the roots of your flowers have the best chance of spreading and finding the essential nutrients they need as they grow. Rocks will prohibit this. They are a barrier to the tender roots of your flowers. Since rocks do not decompose, they provide no nutritional value to your soil and plants. As you garden year after year, it may seem that you are actually growing rocks because they will rise to the surface of your beds. As you come across them, remove them from your beds. You can use them to line pathways, as

decorative elements in a fairy garden, or even group medium-sized stones at the base of a hose spigot to prevent muddy patches from forming.

REMOVE WEEDS

Just as important as clearing the rocks from your garden beds is making sure to pull weeds from the beds. Weeds are plants too, and they will be fighting to access the very things you are providing for your flowers: soil, sun, and water. Even in containers, you will need to remove the weeds that inevitably appear.

As weeds grow, they will compete with your flowers to extract the very best nutrients from your soil. They want the same nitrogen, iron, and glucose that your plant is looking for. In order to provide the best growing conditions for your flowers, get those weeds out as soon as you recognize they are in fact a weed. You may need to allow the weed to grow a little so that you can properly identify it as a weed before pulling it. Some weeds are very similar in appearance to young flower seedlings. In time, as you become familiar with certain flower varieties, you will be able to easily distinguish between a flower and a weed. In container gardens, weeds may become especially cumbersome if not addressed quickly. Weeds, if allowed to grow, will steal your precious container real estate.

It is especially important to remove the weed before it produces a flower and goes to seed. Once a weed has produced seed, it will rapidly reproduce and become more difficult to get rid of. Staying vigilant and pulling weeds as soon as you recognize them as weeds will be beneficial to your garden and save you time in the long run.

If left to grow, weeds will often grow faster than flowers and begin to shade your growing flower, thus robbing them of much-needed sunlight. This will stunt the growth of the plant you intentionally planted in your flower bed. Conversely, if you can keep your garden beds weed-free, your flowers will grow tall and shade the bed, thus naturally acting as a weed barrier to weeds looking for sunlight to grow and flourish.

Sometimes the task of weeding can become overwhelming. If your garden has been overrun by weeds, dedicate a little time each day to pulling them. A little effort each day, spread over a period of time, can produce big dividends.

The Importance of Healthy Soil

Soil is the foundation of your garden. It is imperative that you add organic matter to your native garden soil so that you can create the proper environment for your soil to feed your plants. Don't be stressed about needing to import large quantities of new soil. Start with what you have and add to it. Remember, feed your soil and let your soil feed your plants. As you add organic matter to your native soil, you are building up your soil's health so that it can support the growth of your flowers. Your flower

will draw all of its nutrients from the soil. The more organic matter you put into the soil, the healthier your plant will be.

CREATING MICROBIOMES

Healthy soil provides for drainage and invites the creation of microbiomes beneath the soil's surface as it breaks down organic matter. A microbiome is the vast community of microorganisms contained within the soil and contributing to the soil's ecosystem. These microorganisms handle nutrient recycling, protect the soil structure, and help with pathogen suppression.

Your soil microbiome is made up of a variety of microorganisms that contribute to the health of your soil. As you feed your soil, beneficial bacteria, fungi, and organisms are created in the soil. These microorganisms aid in breaking down the organic matter present in the soil so that it can be used by your plant as food and energy.

Beneficial microbes have a mutually beneficial relationship with plants. These microbes attach to the roots of the plants and eat the materials released by the roots. Once they break down this material, it is fed back to the plant in a form that the plant is better able to access. As you continue to build this microbiome, it is important to use organic means of pest control so you don't destroy what you have worked so hard to establish. Remember, don't treat your soil like dirt!

HEALTHY SOIL AS NATURAL PEST CONTROL

The healthier your soil, the healthier your plant. Healthy soil will even act as a pest deterrent. How is this possible? When a plant is healthy, it is much less likely to attract pests because it is drawing everything it needs from the soil. When a plant is weak and is not able to fortify itself through the nutrients in the soil, it leaks simple

sugars and incomplete proteins onto the surface of the leaves and stems. Bugs will be attracted to these unhealthy plants and feed on the leaves. These bugs are in fact performing their duty in cleaning up suffering plants. When a plant is healthy, all these sugars and amino acids are contained within the plant as it uses them to thrive, thus warding off any unwanted predators.

BUILDING YOUR SOIL

Now that you know the importance of healthy soil as a foundation for your flower garden, how do you get there? One of the best ways to establish a beneficial foundation is by adding fresh compost to your garden bed. Compost is the matter produced from the process of turning organic waste into natural fertilizer through decomposition. Compost is added to soil to enrich and enhance its growing capabilities as it contains many of the desired nutrients plants need. You can create your own compost or purchase some through garden centers, landscape companies, or your city's green waste program where available.

You can also create your own soil mix by following this simple recipe. Since you will probably be creating in a large volume, lay out a tarp on your lawn or driveway and create your mix on top of it, using a shovel or pitchfork to mix everything.

BASIC SOIL MIX

- 2 parts compost
- 1 part vermiculite
- 1 part coconut coir*
  (measured by volume, not weight)

Planting in Containers

When you plant in containers, you should be especially aware of the condition of your soil. Since you are planting in a confined space, you will need to enrich, and even replace, your soil more frequently. The soil in your container should be completely replaced every 12–18 months. Since container-grown plants deplete the soil faster than plants that are planted in the ground, you should also fertilize your plants at least monthly.

As you plant in containers, make sure that they have proper drainage. If you find a container you love, but it has no drainage hole, there are a few things you can do. First, determine if you can drill a hole in the container without breaking the container. Often, you can drill a hole in plastic containers if you are careful. Sometimes you can even drill a hole in terra-cotta, stone, or concrete pots. Second, you can plant your plant in a pot that has drainage, and then place that pot inside the container without drainage that you love. If you choose to do this, be sure that the pot your plant is planted in is smaller than the decorative pot and is easy to remove for watering. Remove your pot to water it and let it drain, then replace it in its decorative pot.

Often, people add rocks to the bottoms of their containers to promote drainage. The truth is that putting this layer of rock in the bottom of your planter actually inhibits drainage and can be detrimental to the health of your plant. When you water your plant, gravity pulls the water down to the lowest level, thus leaving the bottom soil the wettest. When you add a rock layer, you are essentially raising your bottom soil level and bringing that wet soil closer to the roots of your plant. When your roots are left to be nearer to the wettest soil, the chance of them rotting increases. One way to promote drainage without adding rocks to the bottom is to mix perlite in with your soil. Perlite is a naturally occurring mineral that is added to garden soil to improve aeration, water retention, and drainage.

Select a container big enough to accommodate the established root of the plant and be prepared to plant in a larger container if needed as the plant grows. As mentioned, container-grown plants deplete the soil faster than plants in the ground, so make sure you fertilize the plant as needed. Container-grown plants also need more frequent watering than those planted in the ground.

— Chapter 4 —

Planting Seeds

Now that you have taken the time to carefully consider your garden and get everything set up properly, it is time to start planting. Learning the fundamentals of seed starting and direct sowing seeds is essential to the success of your garden. You may find that you prefer one method over the other, but you may also notice that in order for some plants to truly succeed, you must employ a certain method. This chapter discusses how to determine your growing windows by calculating the frost dates, or the average date of the first (occurs in fall) or last (occurs in spring) freeze in your growing area. You will also learn the different methods of starting seeds and how to determine which works best in different situations.

Growing at the Right Time

As discussed in Chapter 1, it is vital to plant at the right time for your growing zone. One of the most helpful tools in determining what can successfully be planted at any given time in your area is your local extension planting calendar. Contact your local county extension office to find a planting guide for your area. If there is no extension office in your area, contact a local grower or nursery to obtain a reliable guide.

FROST DATES

It is vital to know the first and last frost dates for your area. You will notice that seed packets almost always instruct you to start sowing seeds according to frost dates. You can determine the first and last frost dates in your area by visiting www.almanac.com/gardening/frostdates and then entering your city and state or zip code. Your first and last frost dates will then be generated. The period of time between these dates is your growing season. To know if it is the appropriate time to plant your seed, take that important frost date and count backward the designated number of weeks specified on your seed packet to know exactly when to plant that seed. The goal is to make sure that the plant has ample time to reach maturity (the period of time from when a seed is sown until a plant flowers or produces fruit) and then some before your first frost.

LOCAL USDA HARDINESS ZONE

Knowing your local hardiness zone, or the geographical area where certain plants perform the best for that particular climate, is key to selecting plants that will survive and thrive in your area. The USDA Plant Hardiness Zone Map is the standard by which gardeners are able to determine which plants are able to grow and thrive in their region. This system separates the United States into thirteen growing zones by lowest annual temperature to determine where plants will grow best. Plants that are not fit for your zone will not thrive in your garden or are not hardy for that zone. The term *hardy* refers to a plant's ability to survive particular growing conditions, whether they be heat, cold, drought, wind, and so on.

Advanced gardeners can sometimes create a special microclimate, or the weather conditions of a very small section of space that differs from the weather conditions of the surrounding area, to sustain them or to adjust the growing season and have success with certain plants. As you begin gardening, however, it is important to pay close attention to your hardiness zone. You can find out your hardiness zone by visiting https://planthardiness.ars.usda.gov/ and then entering your address.

Starting Seeds Indoors versus Direct Sowing Seeds

Once you have determined your planting times, frost dates, and growing zone, you can choose what you want to plant. When gardening, you will most often be planting from seed, bulb, corm, rhizome, or transplant.

SEEDS are the embryonic stage of a plant.

BULBS are plants that store their energy in an underground globe-like structure. Typically perennials, this plant will grow and bloom for a season and then go dormant, saving its stored-up energy for the next growing season.

CORMS are solid tissue "seeds" that store energy for a plant to access for growing the following season.

RHIZOMES are fleshy underground stems that grow horizontally.

Most often when you start a plant indoors it will be started from seed. One of the biggest questions people have is whether they should start their seeds directly in the garden or inside their home. There are advantages to both, and sometimes your climate may necessitate one method over the other. Often, seed packets and their growing information will tell you if it is better to start the seed indoors or to direct sow. Taking the time to figure out which method works best with each plant and journaling your results can be beneficial as you make plans for planting year after year.

DIRECT SOWING SEEDS

Planting seeds directly into the soil in your garden or container is known as direct sowing. There are many benefits to this method of growing. When you direct sow your seeds, you save money by not having to purchase transplants. Direct-sown seeds become accustomed to the climate, so they don't need to be hardened off like transplants might and they won't experience transplant shock. (Hardening off is the gradual process of a plant becoming acclimated to its permanent growing conditions and locations over a period of time.)

Some of the cons to direct sowing are that you might experience uneven germination. If this occurs, you may have to sow more seeds to account for the loss. You will also need to thin your plants after they germinate to ensure that you have adequate room for the growing needs of the plant.

HOW TO DIRECT SOW SEEDS

You should have your garden bed prepared and ready to go before you plant your seeds. Follow these steps to direct sow your seeds:

1 Gather your planting supplies:

- Seed packet
- Dibbler (a pointed tool used for creating holes in soil for the planting of seeds, transplants, or bulbs) or garden trowel
- Gloves
- Watering can or hose
- Garden hoe

2 Plant seeds according to the directions on the seed packet. Some seeds require light to germinate, and some seeds should be covered or buried in soil to germinate. Typically, small seeds are covered with a light dusting of soil or vermiculite (a mineral that is added to soil or sprinkled on top of soil to aid in the retention of water), while larger seeds are planted deeper. If there are no depth instructions included, a good rule is to plant at a depth twice the size of the seed or bulb.

3 Gently water your seed. Depending on the type of seed and the temperature, it may take as little as 3 days or up to 14 days to germinate. The most important thing is to ensure that your seeds stay moist so that they will germinate. This may require watering your seeds multiple times a day. Remember, a dry seed is a dead seed. You will know you have achieved germination when you can see even the slightest growth above ground. Once your seed has germinated, water daily to allow it to become established (usually 7–10 days) and then follow the watering guidelines in Chapter 2. Newly germinated seedlings are not strong enough to go long periods

of time without water, so closely monitor the surrounding soil.

4 Consider adding mulch (a layer of material spread across the surface of the soil to protect, insulate, or aid in water retention) to your garden beds once your seedlings have developed true leaves (the leaves that emerge after the initial leaves that appear at the time of germination). True leaves are able to perform photosynthesis. Mulch will help to retain moisture in the soil and provide nutrients as the mulch decomposes. Adding mulch to the top of a potted plant will help to retain moisture, prevent wind erosion by holding the soil in place, prevent soil from splashing onto the plant or outside of the container when watered, and add a finishing touch to the container.

STARTING SEEDS INDOORS

When you start seeds indoors, you extend your growing season. In areas with a short growing season, starting seeds indoors extends the possibilities for certain plants and allows you to control the growing conditions of your plant.

Starting your own seeds indoors and then planting them as transplants into your garden or container saves money over purchasing transplants. Another benefit of growing your own transplants is that you are able to grow many different varieties of flowers. Typically, garden centers sell the most common varieties and do so year after year. Purchasing seeds through garden catalogs and online and then growing your own transplants gives you the opportunity to try many different types of flowers.

As you start your own seeds and grow your own transplants, you will know exactly how many plants you need to grow to fill your space and you can grow accordingly. You should sow a few more seeds than you actually need so you can account for any seeds that don't germinate or plants that you might lose in the process, plus any that you might want to share with friends and neighbors.

A benefit to starting plants indoors is that once you plant your transplant in your garden, it is a guaranteed plant as long as you take care of it properly. Whereas on the other hand, sometimes a seed that is direct sown doesn't germinate or dies shortly after germinating, thus leaving a hole in your garden bed if not resown.

A transplanted plant also matures more quickly, thus producing blooms sooner than a seed that was sown directly. In this case, you are able to achieve a colorful garden faster than if you had planted everything from seed. Since your flowers will bloom sooner, you will be able to harvest them sooner and bring them inside to enjoy. You will also be able to enjoy their color in the garden a little longer than if you had direct sown the seeds.

HOW TO PLANT SEEDS INDOORS

Successful indoor seed germination is best achieved when you have a dedicated space for germinating seeds. Before you begin planting, prepare an area in your home, workshop, greenhouse, or even your garage where you can place your seeds to germinate and grow undisturbed over the next 6–8 weeks. Then follow these steps:

1 Gather the following supplies needed for starting seeds:

- Clean seed trays (dome cover optional)
- Seed-starting soil
- Spray bottle
- Seed packets
- Vermiculite
- Gloves
- Labels
- Overhead grow light
- Fan (optional)
- Heat mat (optional)

2 Fill trays with a moist seed-starting soil mix that compacts together in clumps when squeezed into a ball without water running out.

3 Follow packet instructions to sow seeds. Some seeds require light to germinate, and some seeds should be covered or buried in soil to germinate. Typically, small seeds are covered with a light dusting of soil or vermiculite, while larger seeds are planted deeper. If there are no depth instructions included, a good rule is to plant at a depth twice the size of the seed. It is a good idea to sow seeds of the same flower in the same tray, as they will grow at the same rate and their needs will be the same.

4 Label your plants as you sow the seeds. As your seeds germinate, many will look the same. Labeling as you plant will remove the guesswork as your plants grow, and you will know exactly what you have.

5 Keep seeds moist and warm to germinate. A dry seed is a dead seed. Most seeds require temperatures of 65°F–75°F to germinate. If a cover dome is used, remove it immediately after seedlings sprout to promote good airflow. If using a heat mat, remove seed tray from heat mat as soon as you notice that 50 percent of the seeds have germinated.

6 Provide plenty of light (12–16 hours a day). Use grow lights, regular fluorescent bulbs, or a greenhouse to provide light. Your light source should be no more than 2" above your growing plant at all times. You will need to be able to raise it as your plant grows. Rotate seedlings daily and water properly to prevent seedlings from stretching too far

in the same direction and getting leggy. A seedling or plant becomes leggy when it has grown extremely tall with few leaves. This is an indication of the plant needing a closer light source.

7 Ensure proper airflow a few hours each day to strengthen stems and leaves and to prevent disease. Utilize a small fan or window that provides gentle breeze-force wind.

8 When the seedling is ready to be planted, harden off plants once the risk of frost is gone by moving seedlings outdoors for a few hours each day. First, place in a shaded area, then increase time outside by a few hours each day while increasing exposure to sun, and finally, allow seedlings to be outside overnight. Once they have been properly hardened off, seedlings can be transplanted.

Planting Transplants

Once your plant has established three to four true leaves, it is ready to be planted outside. Follow these simple steps to successfully plant your little transplant:

1 Dig a hole that is as wide and deep as your transplant.
2 Carefully remove your transplant from its container.
3 Gently loosen the roots if they are tight or tangled.
4 Place the plant in the prepared hole.
5 Firmly fill in the area around your plant with soil, making sure there are no air pockets.
6 Water your plant, adding soil to any areas that may settle.
7 Mulch around your plant to retain moisture.
8 Water daily until established.

Pay attention to your transplants for the next few days after planting. Sometimes they will experience transplant shock, and you will notice that they are suffering in their new environment. The good news is that with proper care, your plant can recover. One of the biggest factors in survival is ensuring that your transplant receives adequate water when it is planted and for 7–10 days after.

Chapter 5

Caring for Your Growing Flowers

Now that you have everything planted, there are a few things to remember to ensure the success of your flowers. Proper fertilizing and plant care is essential to the health of your plant. Since you know how to feed your soil, these guidelines will assist you in achieving the healthiest flowers and most beautiful blooms. This chapter walks through the elements plants need that are found in the most common fertilizers and how to care for your growing flowers. It will also help you troubleshoot common plant problems and introduce you to pest control methods.

Fertilizing Through Proper Nutrients

As you feed your soil, you are in fact fertilizing your plants. The most common and most essential nutrients for your garden are the minerals nitrogen (N), phosphorus (P), and potassium (K). These three minerals work in tandem to produce healthy plants and are referred to as the N-P-K ratio. Although plants use other nutrients in their growth, these are the most commonly used. Fresh compost contains these essential nutrients, but you can also use bagged fertilizers to nourish your soil.

You can purchase premixed bagged fertilizers with these three important minerals at your garden center. On a bag or bottle of fertilizer, you may notice it has three numbers separated by dashes. These are numerical representations, by weight, of the percentage of nitrogen (N), phosphorus (P), and potassium (K) present in that particular mix. For example, a 100-pound bag of fertilizer with the numbers 12-3-10 on its label is composed of 12 percent N, 3 percent P, and 10 percent K for a total of 25 percent of the bag's weight. The remaining 75 percent of the bag's weight is comprised of fillers, such as sand, limestone, ground corncobs, sawdust, or other materials that help to make the distribution of the fertilizer easier without adversely affecting your plant. Remember, when applying fertilizer, always follow the recommended application rate listed on the bag or container.

NITROGEN

Nitrogen is the first number that is listed in a fertilizer formula. It plays a critical role in producing green leaves and strong stems. Nitrogen is important because it is a significant element of the chlorophyll molecule. Chlorophyll is the compound found in plants that accounts for their green color and allows them to absorb energy from the sun. Plants absorb more nitrogen than any other element. Fertilizers that are high in nitrogen are manure, ammonium sulfate, feather meal, blood meal, and fish emulsion.

PHOSPHORUS

Phosphorus, the second number listed in a fertilizer formula, plays a key role in photosynthesis as it helps to transform energy to make it usable for the plant. Photosynthesis is the process by which plants convert light energy to chemical energy. Water and carbon dioxide combine to form carbohydrates that provide the plant with energy and release oxygen. A plant needs phosphorus from the time it begins as a seed all the way through to harvest. Primarily, phosphorus contributes to the development of strong roots. It also improves flower formation and seed production. Fertilizers that are high in phosphorus are bonemeal, rock phosphate, worm castings, and bat guano.

POTASSIUM

Potassium, the third number listed in a fertilizer formula, plays a vital role in activating certain plant enzymes and regulates a plant's carbon dioxide uptake. Potassium contributes to root strength and development, flower development, and fruit production. Fertilizers that are high in potassium are potassium chloride, potassium sulfate, kelp meal, and banana peels.

SOIL TEST

Before you add fertilizers to your gardens, it is important to determine the actual needs of your soil. One way to figure out exactly what your soil needs is to perform a soil test. You can either do this yourself through a home soil test kit or you can have your soil tested by a company that specializes in testing soil in your area. Once your soil has been tested and the results have been recorded, you can ascertain the needs of your soil. When you test the soil before fertilizing, you are armed with information crucial to the health of your garden, and you know exactly what to add to your soil to improve its health.

Testing your soil every few years will help to keep your soil in the best shape for your plants. As you continue to test the soil and add amendments, you are feeding your soil and allowing it to feed your plants.

Caring for Your Growing Flowers

As your flowers begin to grow, it is important to monitor them regularly so you can address any problems as they arise. Staying vigilant in the maintenance of your garden will save you labor and time in the long run and will allow you to enjoy your blooming flowers knowing you are keeping them healthy.

PINCH YOUR PLANTS

Often when you plant a flower in your garden or in containers, your desire is for it to fill a space and become full and beautiful. One way to achieve this is by pinching. Pinching is the practice of removing a plant's stem above a set of two leaves so that the nodes will send out new branches and the plant will become fuller, thus increasing the number of flowering stems on your plant and resulting in longer stems. You should pinch a plant when it is 6"–10" tall, but often you can also achieve this effect as you cut flowers as they bloom. To effectively do this, cut deep into the plant above a leaf set so that you have a long stem.

Be aware that not all flowers should be pinched. Some flowers, such as larkspur, bloom on only one stem and do not benefit from pinching. In fact, if pinched, you may lose the opportunity for that flower to bloom altogether. (Consult the chart in Appendix B to know whether or not to pinch certain flowers.) Another thing to consider for container-grown plants is the amount of space available in the container. If you have planted multiple plants in groupings in a pot, it may not be a good idea to pinch a particular plant because the room may not be available for it to become fuller. However, if you are planting only a few plants in a pot and you want it to fill the space, pinching could be beneficial.

DEADHEAD YOUR PLANTS

One way to guarantee that you have flowers continually blooming on a plant is to deadhead regularly. Deadheading is the process of removing dead or dying flower heads from a plant to encourage continual blooming. A flower's whole purpose is to perpetuate its species. It does this by producing a flower, and as that flower is dying, it produces seeds. Once a flower is allowed to produce seeds, it signals to the plant that it has completed its mission and often the plant will start to die. If you are vigilant and deadhead spent (dead or dying) blooms regularly, you will be rewarded with increased blooms because your flower will constantly be on task to produce more flowers so that it can produce seeds. Near the end of your growing season, allow your flower to go to seed so that you can save those seeds to plant next year.

PRUNE YOUR PLANTS

During the course of a plant's growth, it may have leaves or branches that become diseased or dead. Because you are regularly monitoring your garden, you will notice these areas of concern and you should prune these areas as soon as possible. Pruning is the act of cutting away anything that is dead, dying, or unnecessary to the plant for the purpose of encouraging new growth. If left on the plant, they could lead to the plant struggling or even the death of the plant. In the case of roses, they require a major prune as they are coming out of dormancy. Follow the guidelines of your local rose society to learn the needs of your rosebush.

Troubleshooting

As you care for your growing flowers, you may notice damage to leaves, stems, or other issues that indicate your plant is suffering. It is important to address these problems as soon as you first notice them. Take a few minutes to determine exactly what is going on with your plant by carefully examining it and then take action. Your plant may be experiencing stress due to disease or a pest infestation. The sooner you take care of the problem, the happier your plant will be. Although not a comprehensive list of potential plant concerns, the following charts may be helpful in figuring out how to remedy certain situations.

PEST PROBLEMS

Pest	Characteristics	Signs	Treatment
Aphid	1/16"–1/8" long Pear-shaped, soft-bodied Can be green, black, red, yellow, brown, or gray Look for two tailpipes at end of abdomen	Twisted, curled leaves Yellowed leaves Stunted or dead shoots Poor plant growth	Spray with high-pressure water stream on entire plant, including underside of leaves Ladybugs, lacewings, syrphid fly larvae

Pest	Characteristics	Signs	Treatment
Caterpillar	1/2"–4" long Color range of pink, brown, green, blue, black Spots or stripes Smooth, hairy, or spiny	Holes in leaves Skeletonized leaves	In most cases physical removal is best for plant health Pesticide: Bt
Iris Borer Caterpillar	2" long when grown Adult moth has chocolate brown front wings and lighter yellow-brown hind wings	Holes in leaves Tunnels in rhizome Tips of iris leaves turn brown	Natural treatment: beneficial nematodes Pesticide: acephate or spinosad
Japanese Beetle	Adult: 1/3"–1/2" long Metallic green head and thorax with copper-brown wing covers Larvae: 1/8"–1" long C-shaped white- to cream-colored grub with distinct tan-colored head and easy-to-see legs	Holes in leaves, flowers, and fruit Skeletonized leaves	Physically remove in the morning or evening Check plants daily Plant four o'clock flowers near roses and hollyhocks to lure them away and keep them from harming roses and hollyhocks Neem oil with repeated application
Rose Chafer	Adult beetle: 5/16"–1/2" long Slender, pale green to tan in color with reddish brown or orange spiny legs Short antennae with series of flat, plate-like segments Larvae: 3/4" long C-shaped grubs with brown head	Feed on flower blossoms, especially roses and peonies, causing large, irregular holes	Physically remove

Pest	Characteristics	Signs	Treatment
Slug	1/4"–2" or longer Looks like a snail without a shell Slimy, no legs Brownish or grayish in color Two pairs of feelers on head	Feeds on leaves and decaying matter Dried slime trail	Physically remove Bury small container in the soil with top of container level with the ground. Fill container with beer or yeast and water mixture (1 teaspoon yeast to 3 ounces water). Keep liquid 1" below top of container. Slugs will be attracted to liquid, fall in, and drown.
Spider Mite	1/50" long Yellow orange with two dark spots, one on either side of body	Webbing on leaves Tiny yellow or white spots on leaves	Spray with high-pressure water stream Ladybugs Insecticidal soap

PLANT PROBLEMS

Problem	Cause	Treatment
Black Spot Leaves turning yellow and falling off	Cool, moist weather Overwatering Lack of drainage	Provide 6 hours sunlight Improve air circulation by pruning or thinning Clean up fallen foliage Water at base of plant and not on foliage Cut back on watering if soil is too damp Provide drainage Fertilize
Rust Tiny specks that can be reddish, brown, orange, or purple	Fungus that multiplies in moist conditions	Gather and destroy infected leaves and plants Treat with organic sulfur plant fungicide Avoid getting water on plant foliage

Problem	Cause	Treatment
Powdery Mildew White, powdery deposits on leaves	Water on leaves Densely planted plants Low air circulation Insufficient sunlight	Thin plants to improve air circulation Prune plant Spray plant with mixture of 1 teaspoon baking soda in 1 quart water Discard infected plant Increase sunlight
Stunted growth	Insufficient water Insufficient sunlight Insufficient nutrients	Increase water Increase sunlight Fertilize
Yellow or light green leaves that fall off	Too much water	Stop watering and resume when top 1" of soil is dry
Yellow or light green leaves	Lack of nitrogen	Feed with nitrogen-rich fertilizer

Chapter 6

Flowers for a Beautiful Landscape

ANEMONE

These early spring bloomers are an enchanting perennial flower resembling a poppy and are a member of the buttercup family.

DAYS TO MATURITY 84–105 days

SIZE 6"–18"

DIFFICULTY Level 1: Easy

GROWING SEASON Perennial

Good to Know

This flower is hardy in cold temperatures.

How to Grow Anemones

1 WHEN TO PLANT In zones 7–10, corms (the solid tissue "seed" that stores the energy for a plant to access for growing the following season) can be started in fall and allowed to develop strong roots throughout the winter for a spring bloom. In colder climates, plant from transplant after last frost.

DAYS TO GERMINATION 12–21 days.

VARIETIES TO TRY Bordeaux, Hollandia, Mr. Fokker.

GROWS BEST FROM In zones 7–10, direct sowing is preferred, but can be planted from transplant. In zones 3–6, plant from transplant after last frost.

CAN BE GROWN IN Ground or 8" diameter or larger container.

HOW TO PLANT Soak the corm for 3–24 hours before planting. Plant 2" deep with the pointy end down, 6" apart. After a few weeks, green sprouts will appear above the soil and last all winter until blooming in early spring.

LIGHT Full sun to partial shade.

WATER Once plant is established, provide consistent water to keep the soil moist but not soaking wet, as overwatering can cause roots to rot.

FEED Fertilize when new growth appears and when plant begins to bloom.

CUT FLOWER Yes.

WHEN TO HARVEST Harvest when flowers have opened and closed one time. Cut at the very base of the plant about 1" above the soil.

Tips It is sometimes difficult to know what direction to plant. The corm can be placed in the soil in any direction. Once your hole is dug, you can place the corm on its side and it will take care of the rest through a process known as geotropism. Be sure to deadhead at the base of the plant often to encourage more blooms.

ASIATIC LILY

These perennial early spring bloomers come in a rainbow of colors and are a good choice for people who have a sensitivity to strong smells, as this variety of lily has no scent.

DAYS TO MATURITY 30–120 days

SIZE 18"–24"

DIFFICULTY Level 2: Medium

GROWING SEASON Perennial

Good to Know

Provide protection from deer. Hardy in cold temperatures. Asiatic lilies bloom only once per season. When cutting the bloom, leave a good portion of the stem and leaves so it can generate energy for the next growing season.

How to Grow Asiatic Lilies

A

1 WHEN TO PLANT Plant in the fall to allow for a good root system to develop, as the winter chill aids in producing large blooms.

DAYS TO GERMINATION 3–6 weeks.

VARIETIES TO TRY Lily Allen Popstar, Navarin, Strawberry Custard, Tiny Double You, Tiny Rocket.

GROWS BEST FROM Bulb is preferred, but can be planted from transplant.

CAN BE GROWN IN Ground or 8" diameter or larger container.

HOW TO PLANT Plant flat end down, three times as deep as the bulb in height, 6" apart.

LIGHT Full sun to partial shade.

WATER Water regularly, keeping soil moist.

FEED Top-dress with slow-release fertilizer after planting, or feed in early spring with fish emulsion, worm castings, compost tea, or nitrogen-based plant food. When buds appear, feed with a high-phosphorus food or bonemeal to produce bigger and longer-lasting blooms.

CUT FLOWER Yes.

WHEN TO HARVEST Harvest when the first two buds are swollen and colored but not open.

Tips Lily pollen can be a problem when cutting blooms for arrangements and bouquets. To avoid pollen stains on fabric, pluck out or cut off the stamen when the flower first opens. If pollen gets on fabric, simply brush gently with a tissue and place in the sun for a couple hours, and the stain will disappear.

BACHELOR'S BUTTON

Also known as cornflower, these reseeding annuals are especially attractive to pollinators and beneficial insects, even when not blooming, due to the sweet nectar emitted by the foliage.

DAYS TO MATURITY 65 days

SIZE 24"–36"

DIFFICULTY Level 1: Easy

GROWING SEASON Annual

Good to Know

This flower is hardy in cold temperatures and is a generous reseeder. To help control self-seeding, remove blooms as they fade.

How to Grow Bachelor's Buttons

☐ WHEN TO PLANT In zones 6–10, seeds can be started in fall, allowing the plant to develop strong roots throughout the winter for a spring bloom. In colder climates, plant from seed or transplant after last frost. If planting from transplant, sow seeds indoors 4 weeks before last frost.

🕐 DAYS TO GERMINATION 7–14 days.

🌿 VARIETIES TO TRY Black Button, Blue Boy, Classic Magic.

🌱 GROWS BEST FROM Direct sowing is preferred, but can be planted from transplant.

🪣 CAN BE GROWN IN Ground or 8" diameter or larger container.

📦 HOW TO PLANT 9"–12" apart. Direct sow seeds ¼" deep.

☼ LIGHT Full sun.

💧 WATER Water regularly until plant is established and then provide consistent water. Once established, water when top 1" of soil is dry.

⚙ FEED Responds well to liquid fish emulsion applied every 2 weeks during blooming season.

❀ CUT FLOWER Yes.

🌱 WHEN TO HARVEST Harvest when flowers are ¼–½ open.

Tips Bachelor's buttons benefit from pinching when plant is 4"–6" tall to encourage branching and new growth along the stems. Consistent deadheading will result in continual blooms.

BEGONIA

Although a popular houseplant, this flower can be planted outside in shaded beds as well. In warmer climates it can be treated as a perennial, and in colder climates it can be dug up and brought inside to overwinter.

DAYS TO MATURITY Typically 12–14 weeks after planting

SIZE 8"–24"

DIFFICULTY Level 3: Difficult, depending on if you can master the right amount of light and water

GROWING SEASON Perennial

Good to Know

This plant is toxic to pets, with the tuber being the most toxic part. Begonias are deer and rabbit resistant but extremely sensitive to temperatures 50°F and colder. Excellent indoor plant.

How to Grow Begonias

1. **WHEN TO PLANT** Late spring. For earlier blooms, start tubers indoors 8 weeks before last frost by planting 1" deep in moist soil, and water sparingly. Once danger of frost has passed, transplant into garden.

🕐 **DAYS TO GERMINATION** 10 days–3 weeks.

VARIETIES TO TRY Maculata, Wax Leaf.

GROWS BEST FROM Tuber (the storage stem of certain seed plants that thicken and grow beneath the soil; they are often able to overwinter underground and bloom in subsequent seasons).

CAN BE GROWN IN Ground or 8" diameter or larger container.

HOW TO PLANT Plant 2"–3" deep, 12" apart.

☀ **LIGHT** Perform best in shaded areas or in situations with morning sun and afternoon shade.

💧 **WATER** Water consistently, allowing the top 1" of soil to dry out between waterings.

FEED Responds well to liquid fish emulsion at ¼ strength applied every 2 weeks during blooming season.

CUT FLOWER Yes.

WHEN TO HARVEST Harvest when flowers are open.

Tips Begonias can be treated as annuals. Dig up tubers in the fall and allow them to dry out before storing in a dark, dry space until ready to be planted in the spring. Do not leave the tubers in the ground, as they will freeze in colder climates or rot in warmer climates. Deadhead spent blooms to encourage flowering.

BELLS OF IRELAND

This annual boasts bright and cheery upright stalks laden with green bells and a light, fresh scent that create interest and texture in the garden landscape.

DAYS TO MATURITY 90–100 days

SIZE 24"–36"

DIFFICULTY Level 1–Level 2: Easy to Medium

GROWING SEASON Annual

Good to Know

Deer resistant and hardy in cold temperatures. Generously reseeds. Be cautious in handling this flower as it has spiny thorns along its stalk.

How to Grow Bells of Ireland

 WHEN TO PLANT Early spring when soil temperatures are 50°F–60°F. For transplant: Sow seeds indoors 6–8 weeks before last frost.

DAYS TO GERMINATION 12–21 days.

VARIETIES TO TRY *Moluccella laevis*, Pixie Bells.

GROWS BEST FROM Seed, but can be planted from transplant.

CAN BE GROWN IN Ground or deep, 10" diameter or larger container.

HOW TO PLANT Plant 12" apart. Direct sow seeds on top of the soil and do not cover, as seeds require light to germinate.

LIGHT Full sun or partial shade.

WATER Keep soil evenly moist until germinated. Water regularly until established. Once established, water when top 1" of soil is dry.

FEED Responds well to liquid fish emulsion applied every 2 weeks after planting and prior to blooming season.

CUT FLOWER Yes.

WHEN TO HARVEST Harvest regularly, when bells are ½ open, to promote growth of side shoots. Side shoots will not generate in warmer climates.

Tips Benefits from cold stratification (the process of exposing seeds to cold conditions to encourage germination and trigger flower development). Place seed packet in the freezer for 2 weeks prior to planting. Then soak the seeds in water for 24 hours before planting. Seeds can be tricky to germinate, so always sow an abundance to ensure successful germination. This plant also prefers direct sowing over transplanting. If you decide to plant as a transplant, provide a deep container, as bells of Ireland have a long taproot.

BLACK-EYED SUSAN

Also known as rudbeckia, this annual flower is a favorite among gardeners. Known for its bright, long-lasting, cheery blooms that attract pollinators and songbirds to the garden.

DAYS TO MATURITY 100–120 days

SIZE 12"–48"

DIFFICULTY Level 1: Easy

GROWING SEASON Annual or perennial, depending on variety

Good to Know

This flower is hardy in cold temperatures and reseeds. Because its leaves lie on the ground, it is a target for slugs.

How to Grow Black-Eyed Susans

1 WHEN TO PLANT In zones 5–10, seeds can be sown in the ground in fall and allowed to develop strong roots throughout the winter for a spring bloom. In colder climates, plant from seed or transplant after last frost. Transplant: Sow seeds indoors 5–7 weeks before last frost. Do not cover seed, as light is needed for germination.

DAYS TO GERMINATION 7–14 days.

VARIETIES TO TRY Cherokee Sunset, Cherry Brandy, Indian Summer, *Rudbeckia triloba*, Sahara. For containers: Goldilocks, Prairie Sun.

GROWS BEST FROM Transplant.

CAN BE GROWN IN Ground or deep, 10" diameter or larger container.

HOW TO PLANT Plant 12"–18" apart. Direct sow seeds 2 weeks before last frost on top of soil and do not cover.

LIGHT Full sun to partial shade.

WATER Water regularly until plant is established and then provide consistent water. Once established, water when top 1" of soil is dry.

FEED Responds well to liquid fish emulsion applied every 2 weeks during blooming season.

CUT FLOWER Yes.

WHEN TO HARVEST Harvest before blooms are completely open.

Tips Black-eyed Susan stems grow from a cluster at the base of the plant. To encourage continual blooms in the garden, remove faded blooms just above a leaf. For cut flowers, cut stem 2" above the soil just after the petals have unfolded.

CALLA LILY

Although not a true lily, calla lilies are a beautiful perennial addition to any garden. Their upright flower structure helps them to stand out in garden beds and containers, providing ample options for coplanting.

DAYS TO MATURITY 13–16 weeks

SIZE 24"–36"

DIFFICULTY Level 1: Easy

GROWING SEASON Perennial

Good to Know

If growing in colder climates, lift and store rhizomes after the growing season and once foliage begins to die back. In warmer climates, rhizomes can be left in the ground to overwinter.

How to Grow Calla Lilies

C

🗓 **WHEN TO PLANT** In zones 1–7, plant rhizomes in spring when all threat of frost has passed. In zones 8 and higher, plant in fall.

🕐 **DAYS TO GERMINATION** 2 weeks for shoots to appear.

🌿 **VARIETIES TO TRY** Apricot Lady, Black Magic, Black Star, Crowborough, Flame, Odessa.

🌱 **GROWS BEST FROM** Rhizome.

🪴 **CAN BE GROWN IN** Ground or 8" or larger container. Can also be successful indoors in a sunny spot in your home. The variety *Z. aethiopica* can be grown in ponds.

📇 **HOW TO PLANT** Plant rhizomes 4" deep and 12" apart. Once planted, water well and keep the soil moist.

☀ **LIGHT** Full sun in cooler climates and partial shade in warmer climates.

💧 **WATER** Water regularly, keeping the soil moist.

🔗 **FEED** Responds well to liquid fish emulsion applied monthly during blooming season.

🌸 **CUT FLOWER** Yes.

🌱 **WHEN TO HARVEST** Harvest when flower unfurls and is mostly open.

Tips Plant in well-draining soil to avoid disease. If lifting rhizomes for the winter, store in peat moss in a cool, dry place to overwinter. For container-planted calla lilies, stop watering and move container to a dark place once foliage begins to fade.

CANTERBURY BELL

A popular biennial choice for cottage gardens, these sweet bellflowers create the perfect mix of romance and whimsy in any garden.

DAYS TO MATURITY 130–140 days

SIZE 24"–30"

DIFFICULTY Level 1: Easy

GROWING SEASON Biennial

Good to Know

When germinating, this plant requires light. Cover with a fine dusting of vermiculite to keep seeds moist and promote germination. Deer are attracted to this plant, so planting in containers that can be easily moved can be beneficial. Mature plants may reseed.

How to Grow Canterbury Bells

1 **WHEN TO PLANT** In zones 5–10, seeds can be sown in the ground in fall and allowed to develop strong roots throughout the winter for a spring bloom. In colder climates, plant from seed or transplant after last frost. For transplants, sow seeds indoors 6–8 weeks before last frost. Do not cover seeds, as light is required for germination.

DAYS TO GERMINATION 14–21 days.

VARIETIES TO TRY Champion series.

GROWS BEST FROM Transplant.

CAN BE GROWN IN Ground or 8" diameter or larger container.

HOW TO PLANT Plant 10" apart. Sow seeds on top of soil.

LIGHT Full sun to partial shade.

WATER Water regularly until plant is established and then provide consistent water. Once established, water when top 1" of soil is dry.

FEED Fertilize once with a 10-10-10 fertilizer early in the growing season.

CUT FLOWER Yes.

WHEN TO HARVEST Harvest when two to three lower buds on a stem are open.

Tips Pinch to encourage side shoots. Consistent deadheading will result in continual blooms throughout the growing season. Integrate this flower in your garden design to attract hummingbirds, bees, and other pollinators. The bell-shaped flower holds water drops that provide necessary moisture for many pollinators.

CARNATION

This popular market flower with full, scalloped, lacy blooms is making a fierce comeback. This pretty perennial flower performs beautifully in garden beds with its straight stems and long-lasting blooms.

DAYS TO MATURITY 12–16 weeks

SIZE 12"–30"

DIFFICULTY Level 1: Easy

GROWING SEASON Perennial

Good to Know

If direct sowing, sow in early spring when a light frost is still possible. Carnations prefer a rich, sandy, well-draining soil that is slightly alkaline.

How to Grow Carnations

WHEN TO PLANT Sow seeds indoors 6–8 weeks before last frost, and plant outside when all danger of frost has passed.

DAYS TO GERMINATION 7–14 days.

VARIETIES TO TRY Amazon series, Chabaud series, Sweet series.

GROWS BEST FROM Transplant.

CAN BE GROWN IN Ground or 8" diameter or larger container.

HOW TO PLANT Plant 6"–8" apart. Lightly press seeds into growing medium and cover lightly, keeping soil consistently moist until germinated.

LIGHT Full sun to partial shade.

WATER Water regularly until plant is established and then provide consistent water. Once established, water when top 1" of soil is dry.

FEED Feed in early spring with a fertilizer that is richer in phosphorus than nitrogen (e.g., 5-10-5).

CUT FLOWER Yes.

WHEN TO HARVEST Harvest when 20 percent of flowers in cluster are open.

Tips Carnations are edible and have a mild clove flavor. Use the flower petals to garnish salads, desserts, soups, icing, and cold drinks. Remove the petals from the flower base before consuming. To extend blooming season into summer, plant in a location that provides mid- to late-afternoon shade.

CHRYSANTHEMUM

The queen of the fall perennial flowers, these long-lasting blooms typically provide a beautiful show as summer flowers are fading and temperatures begin to drop.

DAYS TO MATURITY 16 weeks

SIZE 24"–36"

DIFFICULTY Level 1: Easy

GROWING SEASON Perennial

Good to Know

Deadhead as blooms fade to encourage more blooms. Chrysanthemums are perennials, going dormant in winter and resprouting in spring. In warmer climates, when plant goes dormant, cut to ground. In colder climates, allow dormant branches to overwinter, and then cut back in the spring.

How to Grow Chrysanthemums

1 WHEN TO PLANT Spring, summer, or fall. Garden centers typically place their best chrysanthemums for display and purchase in early fall.

DAYS TO GERMINATION 7–14 days.

VARIETIES TO TRY Quilled blooms, single blooms, spider blooms.

GROWS BEST FROM Transplant.

CAN BE GROWN IN Ground or 12" diameter or larger container.

HOW TO PLANT Plant in rich, well-draining, fertile soil.

LIGHT Full sun.

WATER Water regularly until plant is established and then provide consistent water throughout growing season. Once established, water when top 1" of soil is dry.

FEED Responds well to liquid fish emulsion applied in mid-spring. During flowering season, maximize blooms by providing a weekly feeding that is high in potassium.

CUT FLOWER Yes.

WHEN TO HARVEST Harvest when flowers are fully open.

Tips In locations where temperatures fall below 20°F for sustained periods of time, it is best to lift the plant for the winter and store in a safe location, such as a greenhouse or inside your home. In areas where temperatures stay above 23°F, leave your plant in the ground and insulate with a protective mulch layer.

COSMOS

Cheery annual summer flowers that bloom generously, even in the most intense heat.

DAYS TO MATURITY 60–90 days

SIZE 12"–48"

DIFFICULTY Level 1: Easy

GROWING SEASON Annual

Good to Know

If sowing seeds to transplant, be careful not to sow seeds too early, or they will outgrow their container before they are able to be planted. Cosmos are extremely sensitive to not being deadheaded. Once they have produced flowers and those flowers are allowed to die on the plant, it sends a signal to the plant that it has created seed and completed its life cycle. The plant will then begin to die. Deadhead to encourage and ensure continual blooms. Generously reseeds.

How to Grow Cosmos

1 WHEN TO PLANT Sow seeds after danger of frost has passed. If planting from transplant, sow seeds 4 weeks before last frost.

DAYS TO GERMINATION 7–14 days.

VARIETIES TO TRY Double Click series, Pied Piper series, Purity, Rubenza.

GROWS BEST FROM Direct sowing is preferred, but can be planted from transplant.

CAN BE GROWN IN Ground or 10" diameter or larger container.

HOW TO PLANT Plant 12"–18" apart. Direct sow seeds 1/2" deep.

LIGHT Full sun.

WATER Water regularly to keep soil moist until plant germinates, then provide consistent water until established. Once established, cosmos require less water than neighboring flowers.

FEED For best results, don't fertilize cosmos as rich soil results in fewer blooms and denser foliage. If your plant seems to be struggling, you can provide fertilizer.

CUT FLOWER Yes.

WHEN TO HARVEST Harvest when the buds are colored but haven't opened yet.

Tips Cosmos benefit from pinching when plant is 12" tall to encourage branching and new growth along the stems.

DAFFODIL

One of the first flowers to announce the arrival of spring, these happy perennial flowers bring a welcome pop of color to the spring garden.

DAYS TO MATURITY 12–15 weeks

SIZE 8"–20"

DIFFICULTY Level 2: Medium

GROWING SEASON Perennial

Good to Know

Daffodil bulbs are toxic and can be mistaken for onions. Store in clearly labeled bags and avoid planting in vegetable gardens. These bulbs will bloom year after year in your garden with no need to dig up and store bulbs.

How to Grow Daffodils

1 WHEN TO PLANT Plant bulbs in fall when ground has cooled and before it freezes.

DAYS TO GERMINATION 14–21 days.

VARIETIES TO TRY Butterfly, Double Delnashaugh, Flower Surprise, Pink Sparkler, Suncatcher.

GROWS BEST FROM Bulb.

CAN BE GROWN IN Ground or 8" diameter or larger container.

HOW TO PLANT Plant bulbs in groupings at a depth three times the height of the bulb.

LIGHT Full sun to partial shade.

WATER Daffodils need ample water while growing, but refrain from waterlogging the plant. Water immediately after planting and keep the soil moist. Continue watering for a few weeks after blooming time; then stop watering and let leaves die back to allow bulbs to store up energy for next year's blooms.

FEED Feed when foliage emerges. For blooms in containers, feed with a high-potassium fertilizer when shoots emerge and then every 10 days through blooming season.

CUT FLOWER Yes.

WHEN TO HARVEST Harvest before flowers are fully open.

Tips Once cut, daffodils emit a toxic sap that can be toxic to other flowers. If using as a cut flower, place them in their own water for 2 hours before adding to bouquets or arrangements to allow stems to callus over. Don't recut. In the garden, allow leaves to die naturally before cutting back. Divide bulbs once every 4 years. Dividing is a method of plant propagation where the plant is separated into two or more parts. In plants grown from bulbs, the bulb often multiplies, and a new bulb is evident. In this case, the bulbs are separated, creating two bulbs.

DAHLIA

The queen of the summer garden, dahlias produce various sizes of knockout blooms all summer long and into the fall in most climates. In warmer climates, they are a late-spring bloomer and a perennial flower.

DAYS TO MATURITY 12–16 weeks

SIZE 15"–5'

DIFFICULTY Level 3: Difficult

GROWING SEASON Perennial

Good to Know

If you desire a specific variety of dahlia, plant from tuber, as they produce exact clones of the mother plant. Dig up tubers and divide after first frost.

How to Grow Dahlias

1 WHEN TO PLANT Plant when all danger of frost has passed. From seed: Sow seeds indoors 4–6 weeks before last frost. In warmer climates, take cuttings from the tuber and begin rooting them indoors 3–4 weeks before last frost.

DAYS TO GERMINATION 7–10 days (for seeds).

VARIETIES TO TRY Apple Blossom, Bloomquist Paul Jr., Café au Lait, Citron du Cap, Ferncliff Alpine.

GROWS BEST FROM Tuber or seed.

CAN BE GROWN IN Ground or deep, 10" diameter or larger container.

HOW TO PLANT Plant 9"–12" apart. Place tuber horizontally with its growing eye up, 4"–6" deep.

LIGHT Full sun to partial shade.

WATER For seeds: Keep moist until germinated and then provide consistent water. For tubers: Start watering after first green shoots appear above the soil, and then water when top 1" of soil is dry.

FEED Dahlias require a fertilizer low in nitrogen throughout the growing season.

CUT FLOWER Yes.

WHEN TO HARVEST Harvest when flowers are almost fully open.

Tips Dahlias benefit from pinching when plant is 8"–12" tall to encourage branching and new growth along the stems. Consistent deadheading will result in continual blooms. Provide additional support by pounding a stake into the ground next to the plant and tying it to the plant with twine.

DAYLILY

As their name suggests, daylily blooms last for just a day, but the perennial plant blooms continually throughout the growing season.

DAYS TO MATURITY 1–2 years

SIZE 24"–48"

DIFFICULTY Level 1: Easy

GROWING SEASON Perennial

Good to Know

Undivided plants begin to produce fewer flowers, so divide plant every 3–4 years for continual blooms. Plant in well-draining soil.

How to Grow Daylilies

WHEN TO PLANT Spring or fall.

DAYS TO GERMINATION 14 days.

VARIETIES TO TRY Happy Returns, Pardon Me, Stella de Oro, Strawberry Candy.

GROWS BEST FROM Transplant.

CAN BE GROWN IN Ground or deep, 12" diameter or larger container.

HOW TO PLANT Dig hole twice the size of the container. Plant in groups of three or more.

LIGHT Full sun to partial shade.

WATER Water regularly until plant is established and then provide consistent water. Once established, water when top 1" of soil is dry.

FEED Responds well to liquid fish emulsion applied three times during blooming season.

CUT FLOWER Yes.

WHEN TO HARVEST Harvest when flowers are fully open.

Tips If using as a cut flower, remove dead petals in your arrangement daily and you may be rewarded with additional blooms. This plant may have more than one blooming season and will benefit from dead leaves being clipped away from the continuous green foliage.

FOXGLOVE

Instantly recognizable for its tall, spiked stalks and bell-shaped flowers, this biennial is a cottage garden staple and excellent pollinator due to its high nectar content, attracting bees and butterflies.

DAYS TO MATURITY 90 days–1 year

SIZE 24"–48"

DIFFICULTY Level 3: Difficult

GROWING SEASON Biennial

Good to Know

Foxglove seeds need light to germinate. This plant is hardy in cold temperatures. Foxgloves are considered a biennial, although some may flower in the first year. Often, they spend the first year establishing roots and flower the next year. All parts of foxglove are considered toxic. If the spent blooms are left in the garden, it will reseed.

How to Grow Foxgloves

F

WHEN TO PLANT In zones 5–10, seeds can be started in the ground in fall and allowed to develop strong roots throughout the winter for a spring bloom. In colder climates, plant from seed or transplant after last frost. From transplant: Start seeds indoors 3–4 weeks before last frost.

DAYS TO GERMINATION 14–21 days.

VARIETIES TO TRY Camelot series, Dalmatian Peach, Pam's Choice, Pink Gin, Sugar Plum.

GROWS BEST FROM Seed or transplant.

CAN BE GROWN IN Ground or deep, 10" diameter or larger container.

HOW TO PLANT Plant 12" apart. Direct sow seeds and do not cover, as seeds need light to germinate.

LIGHT Full sun to partial shade.

WATER Water regularly until plant is established and then provide consistent water. Once established, water when top 1" of soil is dry.

FEED If planted in nutrient-rich soil, foxgloves need little to no fertilizing. Avoid nitrogen-rich fertilizers.

CUT FLOWER Yes.

WHEN TO HARVEST Harvest when the first flower at the base of the stem opens.

Tips If plant becomes heavy, add a stake or spike next to the flowering stalk and tie it with twine to provide added support. For additional blooms, cut the center flowering stalk close to the ground to encourage further stalk development.

FREESIA

Highly scented perennial flower that blooms in early spring and throughout summer in milder climates. These beautiful blooms can last up to 3 weeks in the vase!

DAYS TO MATURITY 110–120 days

SIZE 12"–24"

DIFFICULTY Level 1–2: Easy to Medium

GROWING SEASON Perennial

Good to Know

This flower can be susceptible to colder temperatures. Dig up corms for winter storage, and store in a paper bag in 80°F temperatures with humidity between 75–80 percent for 14–20 weeks. In zones 9–10, corms may be left in the ground.

How to Grow Freesias

1 WHEN TO PLANT In zones 9–10, corms can be planted in fall and allowed to develop strong roots throughout the winter for a spring bloom. In colder climates, plant after last frost in the spring.

DAYS TO GERMINATION 12–14 days.

VARIETIES TO TRY Double Volcano, Golden Passion, Oberon, Speedy White, Vienna.

GROWS BEST FROM Corm.

CAN BE GROWN IN Ground or 8" diameter or larger container.

HOW TO PLANT Plant corms 2" deep and 2"–3" apart.

LIGHT Full sun to partial shade.

WATER Water regularly until plant is established and then provide consistent water. Once established, water when top 1" of soil is dry. Stop watering when foliage begins to wither and/or turn yellow.

FEED Fertilize with a balanced fertilizer when the sprout appears and then every 2–3 weeks through blooming season.

CUT FLOWER Yes.

WHEN TO HARVEST Harvest when flowers are still in bud.

Tips Provide support for the stems. Deadhead as blooms die to conserve energy in the bulb for next year's blooms. Divide corms every 3–4 years.

GERANIUM

Popular annual plant for flower beds that can tolerate heat and drought but not frost. These long-lasting bloomers are showstoppers in a border, window box, hanging planter, or as bedding plants.

DAYS TO MATURITY 18–20 weeks

SIZE 12"–48"

DIFFICULTY Level 1: Easy

GROWING SEASON Annual

Good to Know

This flower does not withstand freezing temperatures but will overwinter well in warm greenhouses or homes.

How to Grow Geraniums

1 WHEN TO PLANT Plant outside in well-draining soil after danger of frost has passed.

DAYS TO GERMINATION 7–10 days.

 VARIETIES TO TRY Americana Salmon, First Yellow, Rimfire, scented geranium (for arrangements).

GROWS BEST FROM Transplant.

CAN BE GROWN IN Ground or 8" diameter or larger container.

HOW TO PLANT Dig a hole as deep as root ball and as wide as present container. Plant 10"–12" apart.

LIGHT Full sun to partial shade.

WATER Water regularly until plant is established and then provide consistent water, taking care not to overwater or underwater. Once established, water when top 1" of soil is dry.

FEED Responds well to a balanced liquid fertilizer applied every 7–10 days. Once flowers begin to form, switch to a potassium-rich fertilizer throughout blooming season.

CUT FLOWER Not typically; however, some varieties have foliage that is a popular addition to bouquets and arrangements.

WHEN TO HARVEST For foliage, harvest when stems are mature and not prone to wilting.

Tips Geraniums are beautiful in containers mixed with other flowers. Deadhead blooms by finding the cluster of blooms, following the main stem to the base, and snapping it off. For a fragrant addition to bouquets, try varieties such as Attar of Roses, Chocolate Mint, Ginger, and Lemon Fizz.

GLADIOLUS

Also known as "sword lilies" for the sword-like shape of their leaves, gladiolus are a captivating perennial garden flower, especially stunning when planted in clusters.

DAYS TO MATURITY 70–90 days

SIZE 24"–48"

DIFFICULTY Level 1: Easy

GROWING SEASON Perennial

Good to Know

Gladiolus can benefit from support, such as a bamboo stake, to help them withstand windy conditions. Gladiolus corms can be overwintered in zones 8–10 but should be dug up in colder climates.

How to Grow Gladiolus

WHEN TO PLANT Plant corms 2 weeks before last expected frost.

DAYS TO GERMINATION 3–5 weeks.

VARIETIES TO TRY Black Beauty, Jester, White Prosperity.

GROWS BEST FROM Corm.

CAN BE GROWN IN Ground or 8" diameter or larger container.

HOW TO PLANT Plant corms 4" deep in clusters of three or more 6"–10" apart.

LIGHT Full sun.

WATER Water regularly until plant is established and then provide consistent water. Once established, water when top 1" of soil is dry.

FEED Responds well to liquid fertilizer high in potassium applied when flower spikes start to emerge.

CUT FLOWER Yes.

WHEN TO HARVEST Harvest when half the flowers on the stem are open.

Tips Plant a second and third round of corms every 2 weeks after first planting to ensure a continual set of blooms throughout the growing season. Plant in groups of ten to fifteen corms for a stunning display and to aid in helping stems stand upright.

HOLLYHOCK

This tall, flowering biennial or short-lived perennial beauty provides the quintessential romance and nostalgia sought by many cottage gardeners.

DAYS TO MATURITY 365 days, biennial blooming in the second year

SIZE 3'–9'

DIFFICULTY Level 1: Easy

GROWING SEASON Biennial

Good to Know

Hollyhocks are a biennial plant, often blooming in the second year of growth. They are susceptible to rust, which can be contained to the lower leaves if treated with neem oil or other organic fungicides. Watering from below and ensuring proper air circulation can also help to reduce rust issues. Containing the rust disease to the lower leaves can help it from spreading to the flowers.

How to Grow Hollyhocks

WHEN TO PLANT Late fall or early spring. If planting from bare root or transplant, plant 2–3 weeks after last frost.

DAYS TO GERMINATION 10–14 days.

VARIETIES TO TRY *Alcea rosea*, Nigra, Peaches 'n Dreams.

GROWS BEST FROM Seed or bare root.

CAN BE GROWN IN Ground or deep, 12" diameter or larger container.

HOW TO PLANT Direct sow seeds ¼" deep and 20"–24" apart about a week before last frost.

LIGHT Full sun to partial shade.

WATER Water regularly until plant is established and then provide consistent water. Once established, water when top 1" of soil is dry.

FEED If grown in good soil, hollyhock plants should not need additional feeding for growth. Amending the soil at the time of planting is beneficial.

CUT FLOWER Yes, but wilts quickly.

WHEN TO HARVEST Harvest when flowers are open.

Tips If your garden is in a wind-prone area, the use of bamboo canes for support can be beneficial. Planting near a wall or fence can also give the proper support needed for these tall bloomers. Hollyhocks are a generous seed producer. Collect seeds to share with friends.

HYDRANGEA

This showy perennial landscape staple is also an excellent cut flower that generously blooms from early spring to late fall if planted strategically.

DAYS TO MATURITY 1–2 years

SIZE 2'–6' tall and wide

DIFFICULTY Level 1: Easy

GROWING SEASON Perennial

Good to Know

Hydrangeas do not like hot growing conditions and may be grown in zones 3–8, with some varieties, such as Limelight, growing in zone 9.

How to Grow Hydrangeas

1 WHEN TO PLANT Fall or early spring.

DAYS TO GERMINATION Planting from seed is not recommended.

VARIETIES TO TRY Eldorado, Limelight, Miss Saori, Nikko Blue.

GROWS BEST FROM Transplant.

CAN BE GROWN IN Ground or deep, 24" diameter or larger container.

HOW TO PLANT Dig a hole twice as wide as the root ball and just as deep. Place your plant in the hole and be sure it is level with the surrounding ground before backfilling.

LIGHT Prefers afternoon shade.

WATER Water regularly until plant is established. Once established, water deeply when top 1" of soil is dry.

FEED Responds well to a feeding of a balanced fertilizer (e.g., 6-6-6 or 8-8-8) once in the early spring and then again in the late summer.

CUT FLOWER Yes.

WHEN TO HARVEST Harvest when flower heads are no longer soft to the touch.

Tips Hydrangeas can wilt when cut but can be rehydrated by submerging the stem and entire bloom head in water for a few minutes.

ICELAND POPPY

Iceland poppies are a perfect biennial or short-lived perennial choice for a pollinator garden, attracting birds, bees, and butterflies. These beautifully delicate crepe-like blooms are stunning in bouquets and arrangements.

DAYS TO MATURITY 90 days

SIZE 15"–20"

DIFFICULTY Level 1: Easy

GROWING SEASON Biennial

Good to Know

This flower is hardy in cold temperatures and will generously reseed.

How to Grow Iceland Poppies

📅 **WHEN TO PLANT** In zones 6–10, seeds can be started in fall and allowed to develop strong roots throughout the winter for a spring bloom. If planting from transplant, sow seeds indoors 6–8 weeks before last frost. In colder climates, plant from seed or transplant after last frost.

🕐 **DAYS TO GERMINATION** 14–21 days.

🌿 **VARIETIES TO TRY** Champagne Bubbles series, Colibri series.

🌱 **GROWS BEST FROM** Seed or transplant.

🪣 **CAN BE GROWN IN** Ground or 8" diameter or larger container.

📧 **HOW TO PLANT** Plant 6"–8" apart. Sow seeds on top of soil, as they require light to germinate.

☀️ **LIGHT** Full sun or partial shade.

💧 **WATER** Water regularly until plant is established and then provide consistent water. Once established, water when top 1" of soil is dry.

🔬 **FEED** Responds well to a well-balanced flower fertilizer applied once during growing season.

🍀 **CUT FLOWER** Yes.

🌾 **WHEN TO HARVEST** Harvest when bud cracks and begins to show the slightest color.

Tips Iceland poppies benefit from continually harvesting blooms and will reward you with more blooms. When cutting for bouquets, and before placing in water, sear the ends of the stem with a lighter or open flame for 5–8 seconds to seal the stem for a longer-lasting bloom in the vase.

IRIS

Taking its name from the goddess of the rainbow in ancient Greek mythology, there are over three hundred varieties of perennial iris flowers that come in a rainbow of colors.

DAYS TO MATURITY 16–24 weeks

SIZE 12"–48"

DIFFICULTY Level 1: Easy

GROWING SEASON Perennial

Good to Know

These flowers can be toxic to humans and pets. It is essential to divide iris rhizomes every 3–4 years to ensure continual blooms. Dig up and divide after flowers have finished blooming.

How to Grow Irises

☐ **WHEN TO PLANT** Fall.

🕐 **DAYS TO GERMINATION**
14–30 days.

🌿🌿 **VARIETIES TO TRY** Black
Gamecock, Butter and Sugar,
Japanese, Siberian, spuria.

🌱 **GROWS BEST FROM** Bulb or
rhizome.

🪣 **CAN BE GROWN IN** Ground or 8"
diameter or larger container.

🪴 **HOW TO PLANT** Plant bulbs
or rhizomes 4"–5" deep and 6"
apart in well-draining soil. When
planting rhizomes, position them
horizontally, leaving the top of the
rhizome partially exposed.

☀ **LIGHT** Full sun to partial shade.

💧 **WATER** Water regularly until plant
is established and then provide
consistent water. Once established,
water when top 1" of soil is dry.
Most varieties are drought tolerant
and won't die if deprived of water
for a short time.

⚗ **FEED** Responds well to rich soil
amended with compost or well-
balanced liquid fertilizer. Avoid an
abundance of nitrogen.

✿ **CUT FLOWER** Yes.

🌾 **WHEN TO HARVEST** Harvest
when the colored tip is 1/2" above
the green sheath.

Tips Planting bearded iris, spuria iris, and Siberian iris in the same bed
location will provide a long-lasting display of flowers, as the spuria and
Siberian iris will bloom once the bearded iris is done flowering. Allow
foliage to turn yellow before cutting it back to ensure that it nourishes the
bulb for the following growing season.

LARKSPUR

The versatile, tall, beautiful spikes of larkspur make it a favorite annual flower in garden beds and cut flower bouquets and arrangements.

DAYS TO MATURITY 77–84 days

SIZE 12"–40"

DIFFICULTY Level 1: Easy

GROWING SEASON Annual

Good to Know

Deadhead spent flowers to encourage continual blooms. Larkspur generously reseeds and will come back year after year. Delphiniums are a perennial alternative and relative of larkspur.

How to Grow Larkspur

WHEN TO PLANT In zones 6–10, seeds can be planted in the ground in the fall. In colder climates, sow seeds indoors 5–7 weeks before last frost. Plant in the ground once danger of frost has passed.

DAYS TO GERMINATION 14–21 days.

VARIETIES TO TRY Giant Imperial, QIS series, Sublime

GROWS BEST FROM Direct sowing is preferred, but can be planted from transplant.

CAN BE GROWN IN Ground or 8" diameter or larger container.

HOW TO PLANT Plant 6"–8" apart. Direct sow seeds 1/4" deep.

LIGHT Full sun to partial shade.

WATER Water regularly until plant is established and then provide consistent water. Once established, water when top 1" of soil is dry.

FEED Responds well to balanced fertilizer applied every 2 weeks during growing season.

CUT FLOWER Yes.

WHEN TO HARVEST Harvest when 1/3 of the flowers on the stem are open.

Tips Benefits from cold stratification. Chill larkspur seeds in the refrigerator for 2 weeks prior to planting. Plant in the back of beds for a beautiful backdrop. Excellent dried flower. Allow blooms to die on the stem, and then harvest seeds.

LAVENDER

Beautiful in any landscape, this perennial is a popular herb flower for drying. As an added bonus, lavender oil is a beneficial antioxidant and useful in natural healing protocols.

DAYS TO MATURITY Up to 3 years

SIZE 24"–30" tall and wide

DIFFICULTY Level 1–Level 2: Easy to Medium

GROWING SEASON Perennial

Good to Know

Lavender can be hardy to zone 5. If planting in colder climates, plant in pots and bring into a warm place to overwinter.

How to Grow Lavender

1 WHEN TO PLANT In the spring after last frost.

🕐 **DAYS TO GERMINATION** 14–30 days.

🌿 **VARIETIES TO TRY** For drying: Grosso, Provence, Vera. For the perennial garden: Phenomenal. For containers: Goodwin Creek Grey, Thumbelina Leigh.

🌱 **GROWS BEST FROM** Transplant.

🪴 **CAN BE GROWN IN** Ground or deep, 12" diameter or larger container.

🗄 **HOW TO PLANT** Plant shallowly so the soil line is just above the top roots of the plant. Space plants 24" apart.

☀️ **LIGHT** Full sun.

💧 **WATER** Water regularly until the plant is established and then provide deep watering every 2–3 weeks once the plant matures. Water weekly when flower buds begin to form until harvest.

⚗️ **FEED** Lavender doesn't require a lot of fertilizer but will respond to nitrogen-heavy fertilizers.

❀ **CUT FLOWER** Yes.

⚘ **WHEN TO HARVEST** I larvest in early spring when flowers are about to open.

Tips Cut long stems to bunch together and hang upside down out of direct sunlight to dry. Gather dried flower buds to enclose in sachets for use in drawers to freshen up closed spaces.

LILAC

These tall bushes are a favorite perennial in landscapes for their beautiful foliage and intense fragrance when in bloom.

DAYS TO MATURITY 3–4 years

SIZE 5'–8' high and 2'–4' wide

DIFFICULTY Level 1: Easy

GROWING SEASON Perennial

Good to Know

Lilac bushes need exposure to about 2,000 hours of cold, so they are not suitable for warm climates. Although they can be grown in containers, it is best to plant them in the ground to allow them to develop a suitable root structure.

How to Grow Lilacs

WHEN TO PLANT Early fall before the ground freezes.

DAYS TO GERMINATION Not applicable.

VARIETIES TO TRY Charles Joly, Katherine Havemeyer, Mrs. Edward Harding, Sensation.

GROWS BEST FROM Transplant.

CAN BE GROWN IN Ground.

HOW TO PLANT Dig a hole deep and wide enough to accommodate the plant's root system. Be sure that the top of the root ball is level with the ground surface and backfill with additional compost.

LIGHT Full sun.

WATER Water regularly until plant is established and then provide enough water to keep the soil slightly moist. Beware of overwatering, as it will cause root rot.

FEED Responds well to a balanced fertilizer applied in the spring.

CUT FLOWER Yes.

WHEN TO HARVEST Harvest when ¾ of the flowers on the stem are open.

Tips Plant as a hedge for a privacy screen. Pruning is critical for blooms the following year. Prune after plant has completed blooming.

LISIANTHUS

Resembling a rose in petal structure, lisianthus is a long-lasting cut flower—often lasting 15 days in a vase! This annual flower can be grown as a perennial in warmer climates.

DAYS TO MATURITY 14–16 weeks from transplant; 24 weeks from seed

SIZE 12"–30"

DIFFICULTY Level 3: Difficult

GROWING SEASON Annual (Perennial in warmer climates)

Good to Know

Lisianthus may perennialize in zones 8–10. These flowers can be grown from seed, but the process is a long one. Transplants are preferred.

How to Grow Lisianthuses

☐ 1 **WHEN TO PLANT** In zones 7–10, transplants can be planted in fall and allowed to develop strong roots throughout the winter for a spring bloom. During periods of prolonged frost, provide protection. In colder climates, plant from transplant after last frost.

🕐 **DAYS TO GERMINATION** 14–20 days.

🌿 **VARIETIES TO TRY** ABC series, Arena series, Echo series, Mariachi series, Rosanne series, Voyage 2 series.

🌱 **GROWS BEST FROM** Transplant.

🪴 **CAN BE GROWN IN** Ground or 8" diameter or larger container.

🗂 **HOW TO PLANT** Plant transplants 6"–8" apart.

☀ **LIGHT** Full sun.

💧 **WATER** Water regularly until plant is established and then provide consistent water. Once established, water when top 1" of soil is dry.

🌼 **FEED** Responds well to regular feeding throughout the growing season. Feed with a flower fertilizer containing one and a half times the amount of potassium as nitrogen.

💮 **CUT FLOWER** Yes.

⚘ **WHEN TO HARVEST** Harvest when one or more flowers on a stem are open. Flowers will not continue to open once cut.

Tips Lisianthuses benefit from pinching when plant is about 6"–8" tall. Pinching promotes branching and will encourage more blooms. Deadheading will reward you with a second flush of blooms 1–2 months after initial blooms.

MARIGOLD

This popular annual garden flower blooms quickly from seed and continues to bloom all throughout the summer.

DAYS TO MATURITY 56 days

SIZE 8"–18"

DIFFICULTY Level 1: Easy

GROWING SEASON Annual

Good to Know

Marigolds should be deadheaded to encourage continual blooms. Planting marigolds in and around vegetables can be a deterrent to some garden pests and keep them from feasting on the vegetables. Generously reseeds.

How to Grow Marigolds

WHEN TO PLANT Direct sow seeds or plant from transplant in the spring when danger of frost has passed. If planting from transplant, sow seeds indoors 4–6 weeks before last frost.

DAYS TO GERMINATION 4–7 days.

VARIETIES TO TRY Durango Outback Mix, Queen Sophia, White Swan.

GROWS BEST FROM Seed or transplant.

CAN BE GROWN IN Ground or 8" diameter or larger container.

HOW TO PLANT Plant 6"–9" apart. Direct sow seeds ¼" deep.

LIGHT Full sun.

WATER Water regularly until plant is established and then provide consistent water. Once established, water when top 1" of soil is dry.

FEED Responds well to liquid fish emulsion applied at the beginning of the growing season.

CUT FLOWER Yes.

WHEN TO HARVEST Harvest when flowers are open but still have tight centers.

Tips Pinch when flowers reach 6" high to encourage branching. Plant marigolds around roses as a "trap" crop for aphids. The pests will be attracted to the marigolds and will be less likely to attack roses.

NASTURTIUM

This edible annual flowering plant ticks many landscaping boxes as it is an excellent mounding plant, trailing, climber, container, and border plant.

DAYS TO MATURITY 35–52 days

SIZE 6"–3' tall, with climbers reaching 10' and 12"–24" wide

DIFFICULTY Level 1: Easy

GROWING SEASON Annual

Good to Know

In warmer climates, nasturtium can be a perennial. In colder climates, it is extremely frost sensitive. Care should be taken to protect from frost. Nasturtiums are a beneficial plant, as they attract pollinators to the garden. May reseed.

How to Grow Nasturtiums

1 WHEN TO PLANT Direct sow seeds 2 weeks after last frost. In warmer climates, plant in fall or early spring. For transplants: Sow seeds indoors 3–4 weeks before last frost.

DAYS TO GERMINATION 7–14 days.

VARIETIES TO TRY Apricot (border), Bloody Mary (border/mounder), Orange Gleam (trailing), Peach Melba (container), Spitfire (climbing).

GROWS BEST FROM Direct sowing is preferred, but can be planted from transplant.

CAN BE GROWN IN Ground or 8" diameter or larger container.

HOW TO PLANT Plant 8"–12" apart. Direct sow seeds 1/2"–1" deep. Be sure to cover seeds, as they require darkness to germinate.

LIGHT Full sun, will tolerate some shade.

WATER Water regularly until plant is established and then provide consistent water. Once established, water when top 1" of soil is dry.

FEED Nasturtiums do not require fertilizing, as additional feeding will result in an abundance of foliage instead of blooms.

CUT FLOWER No.

WHEN TO HARVEST Harvest when flowers are open.

Tips Harvest flowers as they bloom for use in salads and garnishes. The leaves can also be consumed. When planted near squash or tomatoes, nasturtium becomes an effective "trap" crop as it can attract squash bugs and prevent them from damaging important vegetable crops.

PANSY

This short-lived perennial flower that symbolizes love and remembrance has a smiling face that is sure to brighten up any garden space. They are especially charming in window box displays and containers.

DAYS TO MATURITY 60–75 days

SIZE 6"–12"

DIFFICULTY Level 1: Easy

GROWING SEASON Perennial

Good to Know

Pinching off leggy growth and regular deadheading will improve the performance of this plant. Pansies are an edible plant that can be used to dress up salads, breads, and desserts.

How to Grow Pansies

WHEN TO PLANT For transplants: Sow seeds indoors 8–9 weeks before last frost.

DAYS TO GERMINATION 4–7 days.

VARIETIES TO TRY Black Accord, Chalon Supreme, Inspire Deluxxe Mulberry Mix, WonderFall.

GROWS BEST FROM Transplant.

CAN BE GROWN IN Ground or 8" or larger diameter container.

HOW TO PLANT Plant 6" apart. Press seed ¼" into soil and cover. Pansies need darkness to germinate.

LIGHT Full sun to partial shade.

WATER Water regularly until plant is established and then provide consistent water. Once established, water when top 1" of soil is dry.

FEED Responds well to a balanced fertilizer applied monthly during growing season.

CUT FLOWER Pansies can be a good cut flower, especially when growing longer stem varieties.

WHEN TO HARVEST Pansies can be harvested at any stage of petal opening.

Tips Placing your seeds in your refrigerator for 2 weeks prior to planting will help to improve germination. Dry pansy petals to use in potpourri mixes.

PEONY

The generous, high petal count and sweet fragrance of peonies make them the perfect perennial addition to a romantic cottage garden design, truly making them the queen of the spring garden.

DAYS TO MATURITY 2–3 years; although peonies may bloom the first year, it is best to wait to harvest from them as they establish a strong root structure in their first 2 years of growth

SIZE 2'–3' high and 2'–4' wide

DIFFICULTY Level 2: Medium

GROWING SEASON Perennial

Good to Know

Provide proper spacing and airflow to help prevent botrytis. Closely monitor your plants for signs of the disease. If infected, you will notice blackened, burned-looking leaves. Take quick action to remove infected leaves and toss in garbage, not compost. In the fall, remove all dead foliage and toss in the garbage can.

How to Grow Peonies

WHEN TO PLANT Fall.

DAYS TO GERMINATION Not applicable.

 VARIETIES TO TRY Bowl of Beauty, Charlie's White, Coral Charm, Joker. For warmer climates, try planting Itoh varieties.

GROWS BEST FROM Bare-root stock.

CAN BE GROWN IN Ground or deep, 24" diameter or larger container.

HOW TO PLANT Dig a hole that is two to three times as wide as the root, and plant so the root is just below the soil surface. Planting too deeply will result in a plant that fails to flower.

LIGHT Full sun or partial shade.

WATER Water regularly until plant is established and then provide consistent water. Once established, water when top 1" of soil is dry. Peonies cannot thrive in drought conditions. Generously mulch around plants to retain water.

FEED Responds well to a well-balanced, slow-release fertilizer once a year in the spring before foliage emerges.

CUT FLOWER Yes.

WHEN TO HARVEST Harvest when flower buds are soft and squishy.

Tips Divide mature plants after 8–10 years in the fall when plant is dormant.

PETUNIA

This no-fuss, continually blooming, prolific spreader and popular annual garden flower is a summer workhorse, making it an excellent addition to containers and window boxes.

DAYS TO MATURITY 56–70 days

SIZE 6"–18" high and spreads 18"–4'

DIFFICULTY Level 1: Easy

GROWING SEASON Annual

Good to Know

Pinching the stems will result in a fuller plant, especially if your plant is gangly. In this case, pinch stem by half its length.

How to Grow Petunias

1 **WHEN TO PLANT** Plant in the spring after danger of frost has passed. In warmer climates, plant in the fall and protect from frost when temperatures fall below 28°F. If planting from transplant, sow seeds indoors 6–10 weeks before last frost.

DAYS TO GERMINATION 7–10 days.

VARIETIES TO TRY Galaxy, Midnight Gold, Superbells, Supercascade.

GROWS BEST FROM Transplant.

CAN BE GROWN IN Ground or 8" diameter or larger container.

HOW TO PLANT Plant 6" apart. Direct sow seeds on top of soil. Do not cover, as they need light to germinate.

LIGHT Full sun to partial shade.

WATER Water regularly until plant is established and then provide consistent water. Once established, water when top 1" of soil is dry.

FEED Responds well to a balanced flower fertilizer applied every 2 weeks during growing season.

CUT FLOWER No.

WHEN TO HARVEST Not applicable.

Tips Consistent deadheading will result in continual blooms. When deadheading, remove the base of the flower to include the seed. Petunias that are allowed to go to seed will slow flower production. For an especially beautiful trailing display, plant in a hanging basket container.

PINCUSHION FLOWER

A favorite option for pollinator gardens, this flower is a champ at attracting bees. Although a smaller accent flower, it makes a big statement in bouquets and arrangements and depending on variety, can be an annual or perennial.

DAYS TO MATURITY 90–100 days

SIZE 24"–36"

DIFFICULTY Level 1: Easy

GROWING SEASON Annual

Good to Know

This flower is deer resistant and benefits from a deep cut into the central stem to allow for branching. Generously reseeds.

How to Grow Pincushion Flowers

1. **WHEN TO PLANT** In zones 7–10, seeds can be started in fall and allowed to develop strong roots throughout the winter for a spring bloom. In colder climates, plant from seed or transplant after last frost. For transplants, sow seeds indoors 4–6 weeks before last frost. Do not cover seeds, as they require light to germinate.

DAYS TO GERMINATION 10–12 days.

VARIETIES TO TRY Black Knight, Fama White, Salmon Rose, Starflower (often grown for its globe-shaped and geometric seed pod).

GROWS BEST FROM Transplant.

CAN BE GROWN IN Ground or deep, 10" diameter or larger container.

HOW TO PLANT Plant 9"–15" apart. Direct sow seeds on top of soil.

LIGHT Full sun.

WATER Water regularly until plant is established and then provide consistent water. Once established, water when top 1" of soil is dry.

FEED Responds well to balanced flower fertilizer applied once a month during growing season.

CUT FLOWER Yes.

WHEN TO HARVEST Harvest when the first 1/3 of the tiny flowers are open.

Tips Consistent deadheading will result in continual blooms. Allow Starflower variety to die back and seed pod to mature, and then harvest seed pod to add to bouquets and arrangements.

RANUNCULUS

This multilayered bloom is versatile in the landscape and makes the perfect cut flower. In warmer climates, this flower can be a perennial. In colder climates, treat as an annual.

DAYS TO MATURITY 90 days

SIZE 8"–18"

DIFFICULTY Level 1–Level 2: Easy to Medium

GROWING SEASON Annual (Perennial in warmer climates)

Good to Know

Ranunculus corms will multiply and should be dug up at the end of the growing season to prevent them from rotting.

How to Grow Ranunculus

[1] **WHEN TO PLANT** In zones 7–10, corms can be started in fall and allowed to develop strong roots throughout the winter for a spring bloom. In colder climates, plant from transplant after last frost.

DAYS TO GERMINATION 10–14 days.

VARIETIES TO TRY Amandine series, Cloni, Hanoi, La Belle series.

GROWS BEST FROM Corm, but can be planted from transplant in colder areas.

CAN BE GROWN IN Ground or 8" diameter or larger container.

HOW TO PLANT Soak corms in water for 3–4 hours before planting to allow them to hydrate. Once hydrated, plant them in the ground at a depth of 2" and 6"–9" apart, with pointed ends down. To plant from transplant, dig a hole large enough to allow transplant to fit in.

LIGHT Full sun to partial shade.

WATER Water regularly until plant is established and then provide consistent water. Once established, water when top 1" of soil is dry.

FEED Responds well to liquid fish emulsion applied every 2 weeks during growing season.

CUT FLOWER Yes.

WHEN TO HARVEST Harvest when buds are squishy and show some color but are not fully open.

Tips Consistent deadheading will result in continual blooms. At the end of the growing season, allow foliage to yellow before pulling entire plant out of the ground. Wash and divide corms and allow to fully dry before storing in a cool, dark place until next season.

ROSE

A staple in any garden, roses come in a variety of scents and forms: miniatures, bushes, ramblers, and climbers. Many of these beautiful perennials are chosen based on fragrance alone.

DAYS TO MATURITY 56–70 days

SIZE 8" tall for miniature roses to 15' tall for climbers, 1'–30' wide for ramblers, 2'–5' for bushes

DIFFICULTY Level 3: Difficult

GROWING SEASON Perennial

Good to Know

Rose care varies from growing zone to growing zone. Find your local rose society and follow their monthly growing, watering, pruning, and fertilizing recommendations.

How to Grow Roses

📅 **WHEN TO PLANT** If planting from bare root, plant in fall or early spring. Transplanted roses can be planted any time.

🕐 **DAYS TO GERMINATION** Not applicable.

🌿 **VARIETIES TO TRY** Abraham Darby, Bolero, Dainty Bess, James Galway, Koko Loko, Lady of Shalott, Wild Blue Yonder.

🌱 **GROWS BEST FROM** Bare root, but can be planted from transplant.

🪴 **CAN BE GROWN IN** Ground or deep, 24" diameter or larger container.

🗄 **HOW TO PLANT** If planting from bare root, soak roots for 8–12 hours to rehydrate the roots. Dig a hole deep and wide enough to accommodate roots. Backfill with soil and water thoroughly. If planting from transplant, dig a hole big enough to accommodate root ball and backfill with soil. Water thoroughly.

☀️ **LIGHT** Full sun.

💧 **WATER** Water regularly until plant is established and then provide consistent water. Roses should be watered to a depth of 2'. Direct water to base of plant. Container-grown roses will need more water.

⚙️ **FEED** Responds well to nitrogen-high fertilizers applied during flowering months.

✿ **CUT FLOWER** Yes.

🌼 **WHEN TO HARVEST** Harvest when flowers are 1/4–1/2 open.

Tips Prune annually to encourage the health, growth, and blooming of your plant. Watch for any dead or damaged canes and prune those anytime you see them, keeping the center of your plant open for ample airflow. Consistent deadheading will result in prolific blooms.

SNAPDRAGON

Performing beautifully in the landscape and as a cut flower, snapdragons provide wonder in any setting. These short-lived perennials are often treated as annuals.

DAYS TO MATURITY 56 days

SIZE 24"–36"

DIFFICULTY Level 1: Easy

GROWING SEASON Perennial

Good to Know

Snapdragons benefit from pinching when plant is 4"–6" tall to encourage branching and new growth along the stems. Generously reseeds.

How to Grow Snapdragons

1. **WHEN TO PLANT** In zones 7–10, seeds can be started in fall and allowed to develop strong roots throughout the winter for a spring bloom. In colder climates, plant from seed or transplant after last frost. If planting from transplant, sow seeds indoors 8–10 weeks before last frost.

🕐 **DAYS TO GERMINATION** 7–14 days.

VARIETIES TO TRY Costa series, Madame Butterfly series, Potomac series, Sonnet series (containers).

GROWS BEST FROM Transplant, but can be successfully grown from seed.

CAN BE GROWN IN Ground or 8" diameter or larger container.

HOW TO PLANT Plant 9"–12" apart. Direct sow seeds on the surface. Seeds require light for germination.

☼ **LIGHT** Full sun to partial shade.

💧 **WATER** Water regularly until plant is established and then provide consistent water. Once established, water when top 1" of soil is dry.

FEED Responds well to a well-balanced fertilizer applied every 3 weeks during blooming season.

CUT FLOWER Yes.

WHEN TO HARVEST Harvest when the first flowers on the spike begin to open.

Tips Consistent deadheading will result in continual blooms. Allow some of the flowers to die and go to seed in order to collect seed for next year.

SUNFLOWER

Often a wildflower, it's not uncommon to see sunflowers along the sides of highways in the summertime. These pretty annual flowers can be planted in succession to ensure a summer full of sunshine.

DAYS TO MATURITY 50–70 days

SIZE 18"–120"

DIFFICULTY Level 1: Easy

GROWING SEASON Annual

Good to Know

There are two main types of sunflowers: single stem and branching. Single-stem sunflowers will produce one flower, while branching sunflowers will produce multiple blooms. Generously reseeds.

How to Grow Sunflowers

WHEN TO PLANT Plant in the spring after last frost through late summer 8 weeks before first frost.

DAYS TO GERMINATION 7–14 days.

VARIETIES TO TRY Double Dandy (container), Little Becka (container), Mammoth, ProCut series, SunFill series, Teddy Bear.

GROWS BEST FROM Seed.

CAN BE GROWN IN Ground or 10" diameter or larger container.

HOW TO PLANT Plant 6"–18" apart. Direct sow seeds 1" deep.

LIGHT Full sun.

WATER Water regularly until plant is established and then provide consistent water. Once established, water when top 1" of soil is dry.

FEED Responds well to fertilizer high in phosphorus and potassium applied every 2 weeks during blooming season.

CUT FLOWER Yes.

WHEN TO HARVEST For cut flowers, harvest when flowers are ¼ open. For seeds, harvest when flowers have died and back of flower has turned brown and seeds are plump.

Tips Plant sunflowers in groups to provide support for each other against wind and rain. Birds love sunflower seeds. To ensure you get the optimal harvest of seeds, cover the sunflower with an organza bag as it begins to die to protect the forming seeds from the birds.

SWEET PEA

The aromatic bloom of this annual flower is enchanting in the garden and as a cut flower in bouquets and arrangements.

DAYS TO MATURITY 70–100 days

SIZE 18"–24" wide and 48"–72" tall

DIFFICULTY Level 1: Easy

GROWING SEASON Annual

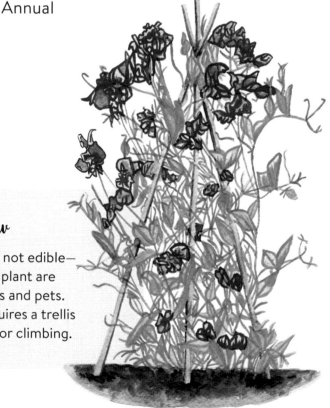

Good to Know

Sweet peas are not edible— all parts of this plant are toxic to humans and pets. This flower requires a trellis or framework for climbing.

How to Grow Sweet Peas

1 WHEN TO PLANT In zones 7–10, seeds can be started in fall and allowed to develop strong roots throughout the winter for a spring bloom. In colder climates, plant from seed or transplant 6 weeks before last frost. If planting from transplant, sow seeds indoors 4–5 weeks before planting outside.

DAYS TO GERMINATION 14–21 days.

VARIETIES TO TRY Charlie's Angel, Jilly, Mollie Rilstone, Nimbus.

GROWS BEST FROM Transplant is preferred, but can be planted from direct sowing.

CAN BE GROWN IN Ground or 8" diameter or larger container. If grown in a container, provide a trellis for it to climb or be prepared for it to spill over, in which case it will need pruning more often.

HOW TO PLANT Plant 6" apart. Direct sow seeds 1/4"–1/2" deep. Seeds must be covered, as they require darkness for germination.

LIGHT Full sun.

WATER Water regularly until plant is established and then provide consistent water. Once established, water when top 1" of soil is dry.

FEED Responds well to potassium-rich fertilizer applied monthly during growing season.

CUT FLOWER Yes.

WHEN TO HARVEST Harvest when half the flowers on the stem are open.

Tips To aid in germinating, seeds may be soaked for 24 hours prior to planting. Sweet peas benefit from pinching and will reward you with more side shoots and blooms as a result. Consistent deadheading will result in continual blooms.

TULIP

For an early pop of color in the spring garden, tulips are an obvious perennial choice, as they flower long before many of their spring-flowering friends.

DAYS TO MATURITY 80–100 days

SIZE 12"–20"

DIFFICULTY Level 1: Easy

GROWING SEASON Perennial

Good to Know

Tulips are mildly toxic to humans and more seriously toxic to pets. Allow foliage to turn yellow before cutting to allow it to nourish bulb for the next season. For longevity in the garden, choose varieties that have been around for a long time.

How to Grow Tulips

WHEN TO PLANT Fall.

DAYS TO GERMINATION Not applicable.

VARIETIES TO TRY Charming Beauty, Red Bright Parrot, Rococo, Yellow Pompenette.

GROWS BEST FROM Bulb.

CAN BE GROWN IN Ground or 8" diameter or larger container.

HOW TO PLANT Plant the bulb 4"–8" deep, 2"–5" apart.

LIGHT Prefers full sun but can tolerate partial shade.

WATER Water immediately after planting, and then withhold water unless your area is experiencing a dry spell. In dry regions, water every 2 weeks.

FEED Amend the soil with a nutrient-rich compost when planting, and then feed again the following spring.

CUT FLOWER Yes.

WHEN TO HARVEST Cut when the first hint of color begins to show on the bud for maximum vase life.

Tips Tulips require at least 6 weeks of cold weather to flower properly, so opt for prechilled bulbs in areas that don't reach the required temperatures. Plant in groups of ten bulbs for a stunning display.

YARROW

With its feathery foliage and flat, umbrella-like blooms, the perennial yarrow plant makes a wonderful addition to bouquets and arrangements and brings a colorful depth to the garden.

DAYS TO MATURITY 120–130 days

SIZE 24"–36"

DIFFICULTY Level 1: Easy

GROWING SEASON Perennial

Good to Know

Yarrow is toxic to dogs, cats, and horses. This flower is hardy in cold temperatures and shouldn't need any protection.

How to Grow Yarrow

1. **WHEN TO PLANT** Direct sow seeds in fall and allow to develop strong roots throughout the winter for a spring bloom. In zone 4 and colder, plant from seed or transplant after last frost. If planting from transplant, sow seeds indoors 8–10 weeks before last frost.

🕐 **DAYS TO GERMINATION** 10–14 days.

🌿 **VARIETIES TO TRY** Colorado Sunset, Summer Berries, Terracotta.

🌱 **GROWS BEST FROM** Transplanting is preferred, but can be planted from seed.

🪴 **CAN BE GROWN IN** Ground or deep, 10" diameter or larger container.

🗄 **HOW TO PLANT** Plant 12"–24" apart. Direct sow seeds on top of the soil, as light is required for germination.

☀ **LIGHT** Full sun.

💧 **WATER** Water regularly until plant is established. Once established, yarrow is drought tolerant and can withstand periods without water. Beware of overwatering, as it can cause fungal disease.

⚙ **FEED** Yarrow doesn't require fertilizing and can thrive without it.

✿ **CUT FLOWER** Yes.

🌾 **WHEN TO HARVEST** Harvest when 80 percent of the flowers on the stem are open.

Tips Consistent deadheading will result in continual blooms. When flowers begin to fade, make a deep cut into the plant as if harvesting for flowers. This will encourage new flower production. Yarrow makes an excellent dried flower. When flowers begin to produce pollen, cut and tie in bunches and hang to dry.

ZINNIA

A summer staple in flower gardens, these generous bloomers are a heat- and drought-tolerant flower. These long-lasting cut flowers are one of the most popular, easy-to-grow annual flowers.

DAYS TO MATURITY 60 days

SIZE 12"–36"

DIFFICULTY Level 1: Easy

GROWING SEASON Annual

Good to Know

Zinnias are considered a "dirty flower" and will last longer in the vase when water is changed daily. They are also prone to a fungal disease known as powdery mildew. Providing ample airflow between plants will discourage an infestation of powdery mildew. Generously reseeds.

How to Grow Zinnias

1. **WHEN TO PLANT** If planting by seed, plant after last frost. If planting from transplant, sow seeds indoors 4 weeks before last frost.

DAYS TO GERMINATION 7–10 days.

VARIETIES TO TRY Benary's Giant series, dwarf, Oklahoma series, Queen Lime series.

GROWS BEST FROM Transplant is preferred, but can be direct sown.

CAN BE GROWN IN Ground or 8" diameter or larger container.

HOW TO PLANT Direct sow seeds ¼" deep, 9"–12" apart.

LIGHT Full sun.

WATER Water regularly until plant is established and then provide consistent water. Once established, water when top 1" of soil is dry.

FEED Responds well to liquid fish emulsion applied every 2 weeks during blooming season.

CUT FLOWER Yes.

WHEN TO HARVEST Harvest when flowers are completely open and flower does not wobble when the stem is shaken.

Tips Zinnias benefit from pinching when plant is 4"–6" tall to encourage branching and new growth along the stems. Consistent deadheading will result in continual blooms. Allow some of the flowers to die on the stem and then drop seeds to sprout and bloom next year.

APPENDIX A: SAMPLE GARDEN LAYOUTS

Putting together a garden plan can leave you feeling frustrated and overwhelmed in one moment and in the next moment be so thrilling you can't stand it. Gardening runs the full gamut of emotions. Good thing there are resources to help you. Here you will find four beautiful garden plans that you can plant in your own landscape. Read about the different possibilities of small gardens and use the suggested flowers and designs to turn a section of your yard into a garden retreat.

Corner Pollinator Garden

More than 80 percent of the world's flowering plants need a pollinator in order to produce. For some of you, the thought of inviting additional pests into your garden may make your skin crawl, while for others, the idea of butterflies, bees, hummingbirds, and more frequenting their garden is enchanting. Whichever camp you belong to, pollinators are so necessary.

Consider turning a corner of your yard into a pollinator-friendly space. By designating a small corner of your space for this purpose, you are placing it out of the way so that you will not be bothered by any bees or other pollinators that might frequent it. You might even find yourself drawn to this space and the activity that takes place there. Here are some things to consider when designing your pollinator garden:

- Plant plants that generate pollen and nectar.
- Plant native plants that support native creatures.
- Plant flower groups en masse to help pollinators locate flowers and to draw them in.
- Provide a water source for the busy pollinators to hydrate themselves.

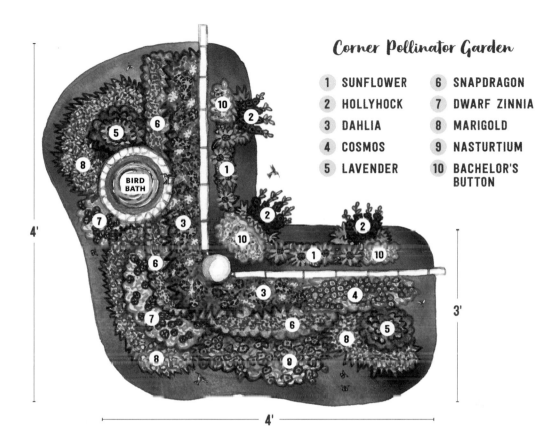

Corner Pollinator Garden

1 SUNFLOWER   6 SNAPDRAGON

2 HOLLYHOCK   7 DWARF ZINNIA

3 DAHLIA   8 MARIGOLD

4 COSMOS   9 NASTURTIUM

5 LAVENDER   10 BACHELOR'S BUTTON

BIRD BATH

4'

3'

4'

Cottage Garden

Cottage gardens provide the opportunity for imagination and creativity. These enchanting gardens should look like they planted themselves and evoke a sense of romance. Arranging plants by height, color, and flowering season draws interest and invites curiosity. Often, herbs are incorporated into cottage gardens, lending themselves to the overall visual and aromatic experience. A cottage garden's less formal, curving lines are an invitation to wander and follow its paths, often ending with a bench or sitting area to provide respite.

In cottage gardens you will find soft, romantic plants with lots of petals along with antique accessories, like well-worn gates and arbors. Along with these elements, decorations such as gazing balls, sundials, armillary spheres, and signs are often included. Of course, if you are planting in a smaller space, individual adaptation will be necessary if there is no room for these architectural objects.

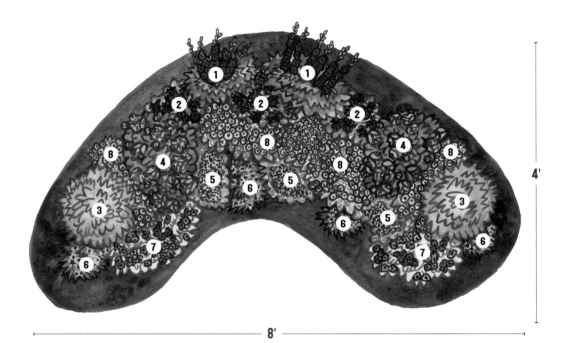

Cottage Garden

1	HOLLYHOCK	5	SNAPDRAGON
2	LARKSPUR	6	PANSY
3	BOXWOOD	7	PETUNIA
4	PEONY	8	COSMOS

Cutting Garden

Often, people are reluctant to cut the flowers in their landscape. Give yourself permission to cut flowers for arrangements by dedicating a portion of your garden specifically for growing flowers to cut and enjoy inside. When planning your cutting garden, incorporate the types of flowers that add interest in arrangements and bouquets. The key elements to a bouquet are:

FOCALS the principal flower in a bouquet or arrangement that the rest of the piece is designed around.

SPIKES a colorful vertical flower in a bouquet or arrangement that accentuates the focal flowers.

DISKS round-headed flowers that fill space in a bouquet or arrangement.

FILLERS the elements of a bouquet or arrangement that fill in the blank spaces or gaps in the arrangement, typically a variety of foliage.

AIR the floral element in a bouquet or arrangement that adds movement to the piece.

You can refer to the Flower Planting Game Plan chart in Appendix B to determine which flowers fall into each category.

When planting your cutting garden, remember that this is a cutting garden, not the focal piece of your landscape. Also remember to:

- Plant in even rows.
- Plant a variety of flowers, including focals, spikes, fillers, disks, and air.
- Plant according to your local growing calendar.
- Start seeds indoors for faster seasonal turnaround.
- Deadhead for maximum blooms.
- Purchase seeds bred for longer stems.
- Feed your soil.
- Save seeds.
- Keep records.

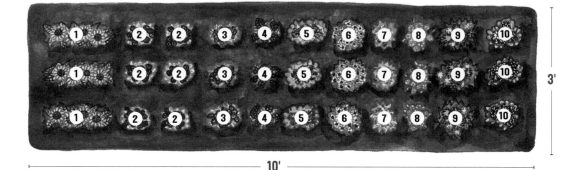

Cutting Garden

1 SUNFLOWER

2 ZINNIA

3 COSMOS

4 CANTERBURY BELLS

5 SNAPDRAGON

6 BLACK-EYED SUSAN

7 BACHELOR'S BUTTON

8 BELLS OF IRELAND

9 DAHLIA

10 YARROW

Drought-Tolerant Garden

If you live in an area that receives little rainfall, consider adding drought-tolerant flowers to your landscape. There are many varieties of flowers and plants that are able to survive on less water. Whether your area receives little water or you are consciously planting to conserve water, there are a few things to consider for your garden design.

In your garden, you might choose to incorporate a few hardscape elements, such as decks, gravel pathways, and patios. As you add plants into your design, strategically construct your garden beds with low spots for planting where water will drain toward your plants. If planted in this manner, in times of rainfall the water will run to the plants and collect in the depression, providing needed water and allowing the plants in this area to be watered deeply. Be sure to heavily mulch your plants to aid in water retention and amend your soil to strengthen your plants.

Keep in mind that although these plants may be drought tolerant, they still need water to survive. Water deeply and less frequently to ensure their health.

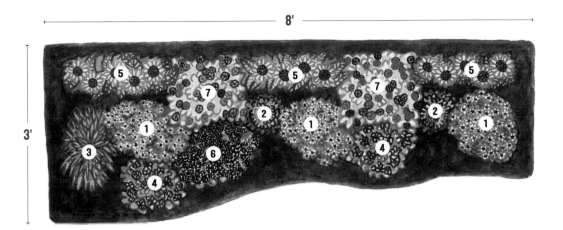

Drought-Tolerant Border Garden

1 BLACK-EYED SUSAN 5 SUNFLOWER

2 LAVENDER 6 YARROW

3 ROSEMARY 7 ZINNIA

4 LISIANTHUS

APPENDIX B: HARVESTING AND ARRANGING YOUR FLOWERS

Harvesting Your Flowers

Now that you know how to grow beautiful flowers, you will have an abundance of fresh flowers to display in your home or to arrange and share with friends. There are a few key things to keep in mind as you cut your flowers:

- Have clean buckets and cool water to place your stems in as soon as they are cut.
- Cut stems on an angle with sharp, clean snippers.
- Harvest flowers at the proper stage.
- Cut the longest stem you can for maximum stem length. You can trim later.
- Remove, or strip off, bottom leaves.
- Allow your flowers to hydrate for 2–3 hours before arranging.

Arranging Your Flowers

One of the best things about growing your own flowers is the joy of bringing them into your home. By following a few fundamental steps, you can create an arrangement you will be proud to display.

1 First, gather your supplies: flowers, water, sharp snips, an anchor for your flowers (floral tape or chicken wire), and a vessel to hold your arrangement. If you have a lazy Susan, use it to place your vessel on as you arrange. This will make designing an evenly balanced arrangement a breeze. Use your imagination when choosing a vessel. A vase, bucket, bowl, pitcher, or even an old urn can be a beautiful way to showcase your flowers.

2 Depending on the vessel you chose, you may need to carefully create an anchor for your flowers so they stay put by using one of the following methods:

- Use floral tape to create a grid across the top of your vessel by running strips of tape ½" apart in one direction. Then tape ½" apart perpendicularly across the other direction.

- Cut a square of chicken wire that is twice the size of your opening, bend it to form a ball, and tuck it into your vessel.

3. Ensure that all your flowers have been stripped of any foliage that may fall below the waterline. Any foliage in the water will decay and shorten the life of your arrangement.

4. Determine whether your arrangement will be horizontal or vertical, and establish your lines by adding your chosen fillers and foliage to create your framework. Place them at varying angles to add interest.

5. Add key focal flowers in groupings or singly throughout your arrangement.

6. Add supporting flowers (disks, fillers, air, spikes) and incorporate accent colors in varying heights to add interest.

7. Rotate your vessel to look for any voids or holes in your arrangement and fill in as necessary. Stand back from your arrangement or view it in a mirror to aid in finding the voids.

8. Display your arrangement in an area away from ripening fruit. As fruit ripens it emits ethylene gas that causes flowers to age more rapidly and makes them more prone to wilt and wither. Similarly, avoid setting your arrangement under air vents and in the direct flow of fans.

9. To prolong the life of your flowers, change the water in your arrangement daily.

FLOWER PLANTING GAME PLAN

Flower	Background	Middle	Foreground	Pinch	Focal	Spike	Disk	Filler	Air
Anemone		X	X		X		X		
Asiatic Lily		X			X				
Bachelor's Button	X	X		X					X
Begonia		X	X						
Bells of Ireland		X						X	
Black-Eyed Susan		X					X		
Calla Lily		X			X				
Canterbury Bell	X					X		X	
Carnation		X	X	X			X		
Chrysanthemum		X		X	X				
Cosmos	X	X		X			X		
Daffodil		X	X		X				
Dahlia	X	X		X	X				
Daylily		X							
Foxglove		X				X			
Freesia			X					X	
Geranium		X	X						
Gladiolus		X				X			
Hollyhock	X								
Hydrangea	X				X				

Flower	Background	Middle	Foreground	Pinch	Focal	Spike	Disk	Filler	Air
Iceland Poppy		X	X		X		X		
Iris		X				X			
Larkspur	X	X				X			
Lavender		X						X	
Lilac	X							X	
Lisianthus		X		X	X				
Marigold		X		X			X		
Nasturtium			X						
Pansy			X						
Peony		X			X				
Petunia			X						
Pincushion Flower	X	X							X
Ranunculus		X	X		X				
Rose		X			X				
Snapdragon		X		X		X			
Sunflower	X			X*	X				
Sweet Pea	X								X
Tulip		X	X		X				
Yarrow		X					X		
Zinnia	X	X		X	X				

*(branching varieties only)

APPENDIX C: RESOURCES FOR ADDITIONAL INFORMATION ON GROWING FLOWERS

Further Reading

Cool Flowers: How to Grow and Enjoy Long-Blooming Hardy Annual Flowers Using Cool Weather Techniques.
By Lisa Mason Ziegler. (Saint Lynn's Press, September 2014).

Floret Farm's A Year in Flowers: Designing Gorgeous Arrangements for Every Season.
By Erin Benzakein, Julie Chai, Jill Jorgensen, and Chris Benzakein. (Chronicle Books, February 2020).

Floret Farm's Cut Flower Garden: Grow, Harvest, and Arrange Stunning Seasonal Blooms.
By Erin Benzakein, Julie Chai, and Michele M. Waite. (Chronicle Books, March 2017).

The Flower Farmer: An Organic Grower's Guide to Raising and Selling Cut Flowers.
By Lynn Byczynski and Robin Wimbiscus. (Chelsea Green Publishing, February 2008).

Grow and Gather: A Gardener's Guide to a Year of Cut Flowers.
By Grace Alexander, Rob Mackenzie, and Dean Hearne. (Quadrille Publishing, September 2021).

Vegetables Love Flowers: Companion Planting for Beauty and Bounty.
By Lisa Mason Ziegler. (Cool Springs Press, March 2018).

The Well-Gardened Mind: The Restorative Power of Nature.
By Sue Stuart-Smith. (Scribner, July 2020).

Online Resources

Floret
www.floretflowers.com
Website with a seed shop and information on growing flowers.

Gardening Know How
www.gardeningknowhow.com
Website providing gardening information.

The Gardener's Workshop
https://thegardenersworkshop.com
Website providing gardening information, workshops, seeds, and gardening supplies.

Growing in the Garden
https://growinginthegarden.com
Website sharing gardening tips and inspiration.

The Old Farmer's Almanac
www.almanac.com/gardening/frostdates
Find the average dates of first and last frost for the United States and Canada.

The Potter's Bench
www.thepottersbench.com
The author's website containing gardening information and inspiration.

USDA Plant Hardiness Zone Map
https://planthardiness.ars.usda.gov
Find your plant hardiness zone by entering your zip code.

Podcasts

The Dirt on Flowers
www.thedirtonflowers.com
Podcast aimed at flower farmers while including general best practices for growing flowers.

Gardening with the RHS
www.rhs.org.uk/about-the-rhs/publications/podcasts
Podcast offering seasonal advice, inspiration, and practical solutions to gardening problems.

Let's Grow, Girls ("Growing Cut Flowers")
www.letsgrowgirls.co.uk/podcast
Educational podcast teaching how to grow cut flowers.

Suppliers

Eden Brothers
www.edenbrothers.com
Wide selection of heirloom seeds and bulbs.

Floret
www.floretflowers.com
Website with a seed shop and information on growing flowers.

The Gardener's Workshop
https://thegardenersworkshop.com
Website providing gardening information, workshops, seeds, and gardening supplies.

Johnny's Selected Seeds
www.johnnyseeds.com
Extensive seed inventory along with supplies and educational information.

Rare Seeds
(Baker Creek Heirloom Seed Company)
www.rareseeds.com
Heirloom seeds, books, and supplies.

Territorial Seed Company
https://territorialseed.com
Supplies and organic and heirloom seeds.

US/METRIC CONVERSION CHART

VOLUME CONVERSIONS

US VOLUME MEASURE	METRIC EQUIVALENT
1/8 teaspoon	0.5 milliliter
1/4 teaspoon	1 milliliter
1/2 teaspoon	2 milliliters
1 teaspoon	5 milliliters
1/2 tablespoon	7 milliliters
1 tablespoon (3 teaspoons)	15 milliliters
2 tablespoons (1 fluid ounce)	30 milliliters
1/4 cup (4 tablespoons)	60 milliliters
1/3 cup	90 milliliters
1/2 cup (4 fluid ounces)	125 milliliters
2/3 cup	160 milliliters
3/4 cup (6 fluid ounces)	180 milliliters
1 cup (16 tablespoons)	250 milliliters
1 pint (2 cups)	500 milliliters
1 quart (4 cups)	1 liter (about)

WEIGHT CONVERSIONS

US WEIGHT MEASURE	METRIC EQUIVALENT
1/2 ounce	15 grams
1 ounce	30 grams
2 ounces	60 grams
3 ounces	85 grams
1/4 pound (4 ounces)	115 grams
1/2 pound (8 ounces)	225 grams
3/4 pound (12 ounces)	340 grams
1 pound (16 ounces)	454 grams

INDEX

ABOUT THE AUTHOR

Stephanie Walker is a mother of three and a certified master gardener in Arizona who specializes in small space, urban, and cottage flower gardening. She is also a garden coach and consultant, as well as the blogger behind *The Potter's Bench*. She currently maintains a small flower farm, growing flowers for CSA flower subscriptions, special order bouquets, and floral arrangements. Stephanie offers consultation services, online and in-person workshops, and more. Stephanie's passion is teaching others about gardening and helping them find success in their own garden spaces. She provides information and education on her website and *Instagram*. Learn more at ThePottersBench.com.

EVERYTHING YOU NEED TO KNOW ABOUT CONTAINER GARDENING!

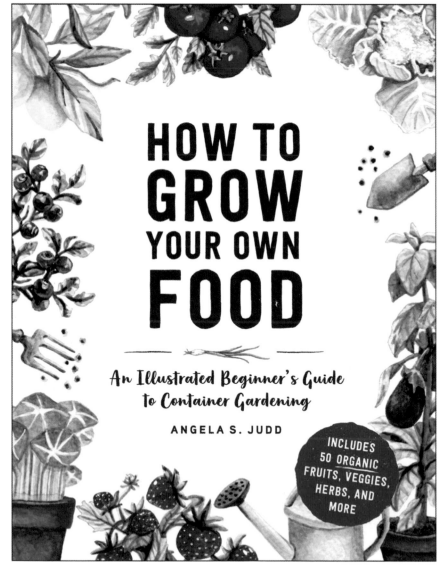

HOW TO GROW YOUR OWN FOOD

An Illustrated Beginner's Guide to Container Gardening

ANGELA S. JUDD

INCLUDES 50 ORGANIC FRUITS, VEGGIES, HERBS, AND MORE

Pick Up or Download Your Copy Today!

adamsmedia
An Imprint of Simon & Schuster